My Journey with ARTJAMILA

(Part 1)

NOORHASHIMAH MOHAMED NOORDIN

Copyright © 2020 by Noorhashimah Mohamed Noordin.

ISBN-13   978-1-6455-0975-2

All rights reserved. No part of this book may be reproduced or transmitted in any form or by any means, electronic or mechanical, including photocopying, recording, or by any information storage and retrieval system, without permission in writing from the copyright owner.

The views expressed in this work are solely those of the author and do not necessarily reflect the views of the publisher, and the publisher hereby disclaims any responsibility for them.

Matchstick Literary
1-888-306-8885
orders@matchliterary.com

To Jamila, her family, people who have been with this journey from the very beginning, people who have witnessed this journey unfold, autistic children and their parents, art collectors, art curators, lovers of art, and the general public.

Preface

Below are the footprints of my journey. The important milestones are highlighted in the footprints for reference by readers while reading this journey. The painting featured on the title page is a painting by Jamila, titled *The Three Ladies*. It is Jamila's unique masterpiece depicting her treasured memories during her childhood with me and my youngest daughter, Jemima, the co-writer of this book.

This journey of discovery is a documentation of our travels for fifteen years, from 2002 through the first quarter of 2018. Our journey will continue in *My Journey with Artjamila, Part 2* at another milestone of achievements.

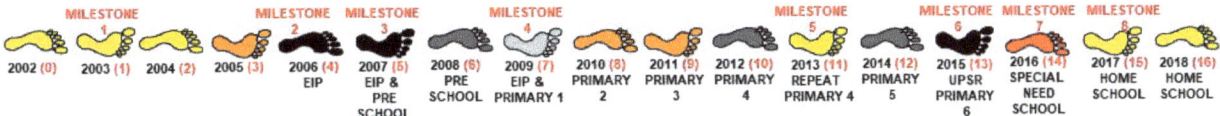

A-1: The footprints of my journey

Introduction

My Journey with Artjamila, Part 1 documents the journey my autistic child and I have taken together. It is a journey of discovery through the experiments I made in teaching and coaching my daughter, Jamila, who learns differently than others and who sees the world from a unique perspective. Since my daughter is a visual thinker and holds information in ways that people can hardly understand and sees things in ways that others might find unimaginable, I had to break from the standard mould of teaching. I learned to adapt to her and not to lead her, as opposed to the approach of current educational systems.

> *If they can't learn the way we teach, we teach the way they learn.*
> —Dr O. Ivar Lovaas

I decided to take charge and make observations about my daughter. Eventually, I create customised workable solutions for my unique daughter with a learning system that is people-centred (humanistic pedagogy, focussing on the emotional and social development of children as part of achieving success, as opposed to the structured system in the school curriculum). I managed to connect and engage with my daughter, and so I began to take a holistic approach. I decided to concentrate with what my daughter can do (her strengths, rather than what she cannot do).

> *Start with what is right rather than what is acceptable.*
> —Franz Kafka

> *The desire must come from the child, not us.*
> —Ruth

I will share a step-by-step journey and highlight all the important milestones of decision-making, sacrifices, and changes of route and directions. I will also show my educational approach, homeschool curriculum structure, the system used in teaching, and educational route showing the many options towards getting to a destination. The fruit of my labour shone like a star when my daughter Jamila managed to sit for UPSR (the government elementary examination) at the age of thirteen in 2015 and become an artist at the age of fourteen in 2016.

My daughter might have developmental and societal behaviour milestones in a different order than her peers, but she is able to accomplish her own victories. One doesn't have to be perfect to achieve big dreams. My child's weakness became a gift, and my daughter is now sharing the pureness of the rhythm of life with the world. The rocky journey in the dark turned into a *beautiful adventure* and a *fascinating experience*. Without darkness, stars cannot shine. We can only see the light in darkness.

This journey has taught me:
1. To see things from a different perspective
2. To learn to look at things/issues beyond what the naked eye can see
3. To get away from the standard mould of teaching
4. That art is a therapy
5. To treasure memories (Jamila has created a unique masterpiece of her memories in the form of collaged events in her paintings. She is telling us that life is all about making memories. Today's little moments become tomorrow's precious memories.)
6. To see the magical strength of willpower.

From being nonverbal, Jamila became verbal. From being completely restless and hyperactive, she became calm and graceful. From being unable to give attention to a task presented, she became able to focus on the tasks given to her more than most people can now, especially when she paints. From not being able to perform self-help skills, she can now even perform household duties and is diligent in performing her daily tasks. From being very dependent on others, she can now be independent in many aspects of tasks and duties. From being in her own world, she can now socialise with people and respond to certain questions well. And finally, from being constantly nervous, she is now more composed than she was before and can take instructions without much hassle. I hope my journey and Jamila's creations of art become an inspiration to others. Life is a journey; enjoy it.

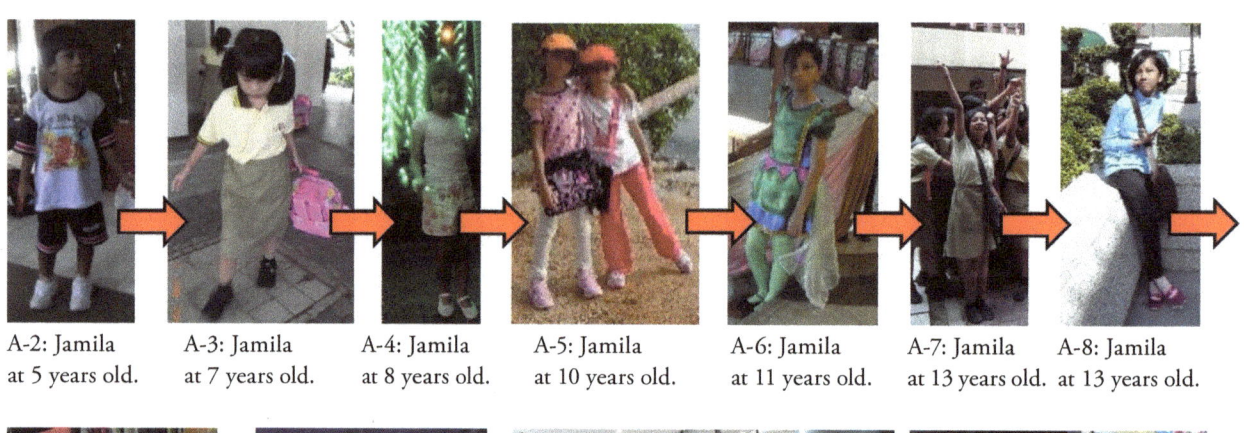

A-2: Jamila at 5 years old.

A-3: Jamila at 7 years old.

A-4: Jamila at 8 years old.

A-5: Jamila at 10 years old.

A-6: Jamila at 11 years old.

A-7: Jamila at 13 years old.

A-8: Jamila at 13 years old.

A-9: Jamila at 14 years old.

A-10: Jamila at 14 years old with the Crown Prince of Selangor.

A-11: Jamila at 15 years old with me at Bank Negara exhibition.

A-12: Jamila at 15 years old.in her art studio.

A-13: Jamila at 15 years old.with Tan Sri Dato' Azman Hashim at Bank Negara Exhibition.

A-14: Jamila at 15 years old.at ArtEDecor exhibition in Matrade, KL, Malaysia.

A-15: Jamila at 15 years old at a charity exhibition by NASOM at Utropolis, Glenmarie, Selangor

A-16: Jamila at 15 years old with Director Securities Commission Malaysia for a charity exhibition.

Contents

Preface v

Introduction vii

    Chapter 1: Early Years 1

    Chapter 2: Primary School Years 5

    Chapter 3: Homeschool: Art as Therapy 20

    Chapter 4: Turning Memories into Masterpieces 43

    Chapter 5: Artjamila's Biography and Achievements: 53

    Chapter 6: Opinions of Artjamila's Collectors 60

    Chapter 7: Opinions of Art Curators 67

    Chapter 8: Opinions of Established Artists 70

    Chapter 9: Opinions of Art Lovers 75

    Chapter 10: People Who Were with Me through My Hardest Times on this Journey 79

    Chapter 11: Conclusion: Words of Advice and the Way Ahead 85

    Chapter 12: Selected Early Years Sketches with Interpretations 91

    Chapter 13: Selected Early Years Digital Drawings with Interpretations..................... 98

    Chapter 14: Selected Recent Paintings with Interpretations 106

Appendix 113

About the Authors and the Artist 123

Chapter 1

EARLY YEARS

Wan Jamila was born in Kuala Lumpur, Malaysia, 13 June 2002. She is the elder of two sisters and has three adult brothers. She looked like a normal and healthy baby at birth and at age one. She was active and attentive at two years old. She had good eye contact too.

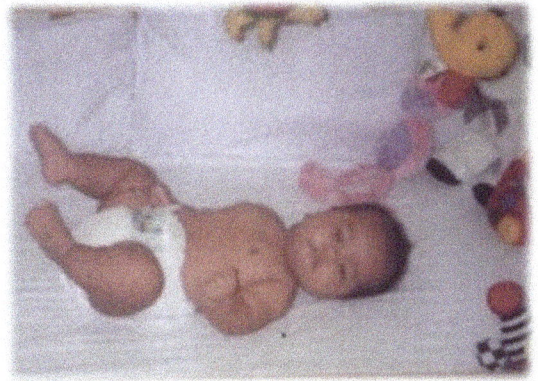
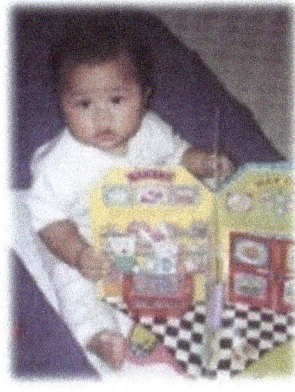
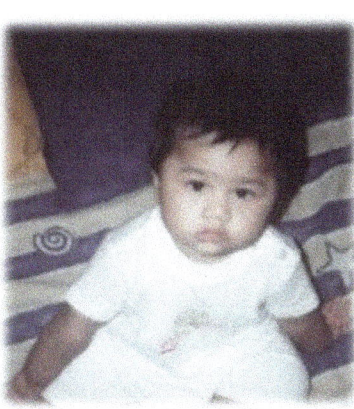

1-2: 1 month old   1-3: 1 year old   1-9:2 years old

Jamila's younger sister, Jemima, was born 18 September 2003. When Jemima was two years old, we started to notice the differences between them. Compared to Jemima, Jamila had difficulties with verbal communication and social interaction. Jamila was then diagnosed as autistic at the age of four. She had lack of eye contact and exhibits repetitive and self-stimulatory behaviours, like humming the same sound over and over and throwing cards in the air. But even though she had difficulties in verbal communication and social interaction, she was fully aware of what went on around her.

At the age of four, Jamila was non-verbal. She used drawings to reveal her feelings of happiness, sadness, and anger. She drew her own interpretation of people with human expressions based on her experiences and observations.

I make art when I can't gather the words to say.

—Nikki Rowe

1-12: sadness   1-14: sadness

1-17: Joy   1-18: Joy

1-20: Surprise   1-21: Boredom

I started my travels with an autistic child in darkness. It was something I wasn't prepared for, and it was a hard and painful journey for me. It was challenging to balance the weight of working a double career as an architect and a lecturer with the responsibility of taking care of an autistic child. Jamila was diagnosed as autistic when I was at the top of my profession.

1-23: As a Lecturer (Associate Professor) in a Local University (UiTM):

1-24: As Speaker at Institute of Architects Malaysia (PAM) for Part III Professional Examination Workshop

1-25: As LAM Part III Professional Examination Committee:

1-26: As a Principal to an architectural practice firm (Noorhashima.n,Noordin Architect)

1-27: Managing projects and managing a sole proprietor company.

1-28: Managing projects and managing a sole proprietor company.

Jamila went through various early-intervention programs as soon as her condition was diagnosed. She was sent to an autism therapy centre that provided occupational therapy to develop her self-help skills and reduce autistic-featured behaviours. The centre also taught Jamila how to function like other children. She received speech therapy to develop verbal communication. We saw some improvement in her, especially on sensory issues, but she remained stagnant after a period of therapy. When Jamila was five years old, in 2007, we decided to send her to a traditional kindergarten in hopes she would develop and blend in with the "normal" children there. We were lucky to have understanding and caring kindergarten teachers. With their good care and guidance and the consistent home-applied behaviour analysis (ABA programme), Jamila reduced her unwanted behaviours and increased her initiation with the surrounding environment. But she remained non-verbal. We sought advice from a paediatrician, and it was recommended we move her to a language enrichment and stimulation centre, which offered language enhancement and stimulation training for children with special needs. There, Jamila learned to recognise facial expressions and started to utter single words.

1-29: Dr. Norizan Rajak (Early Intervention Centre, Selangor).

I had the honour of being among the first of Jamila's playmates in 2008, when she was age six. Her favourite game was singing and playing "patty-cake, patty-cake". She also enjoyed sensory "artwork" using foam to develop reciprocity and turn taking in play. I still remember how surprised she was when I sprayed the foam on the table. We started doodling on it, and she would laugh at my attempt to draw. That sense of humour developed well, and she started to initiate games that she enjoyed and learned. Jamila is a joyful and free-spirited girl who is set to soar to the best of her potentials. Arts is her language to communicate to the world, and I hope there will be many good "listeners" out there who are ready to be engaged as well.

—Dr Norizan Rajak

Parallel to the intervention at the language enhancement center, Jamila continued her presence at the kindergarten with periodic monitoring services provided by the therapy center.

1-30: Jamila at preschool in 2008 when she was 6 years old

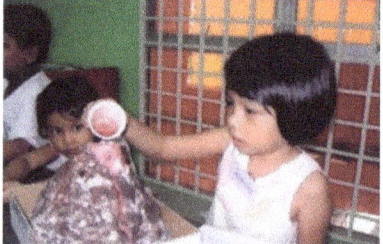

1-31: Jamila at preschool in 2008 when she was 6 years old

1-32: Jamila at preschool in 2008 when she was 6 years old

1-33: Jamila at preschool in 2008 when she was 6 years old

Chapter 2
PRIMARY SCHOOL YEARS

At seven years old, Jamila went to a private primary school with a support teacher until standard 3 (2009–2011).

It is not the 'differently able', but the attitude of the normal to the 'differently able' is the hardest thing to bear. Every child should be given a chance. Nothing is impossible to achieve. Seek and you will find.

—Mr Lee Peng Chiong

2-1: Mr. Lee Peng Chiong (Principal Sri Acmar Primary school)

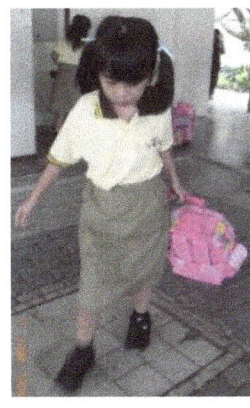  

2-3: Standard 1 (2008) Primary School   2-5: Standard 1 (2008) Primary School   2-8: Standard 1 (2008) Primary School

2-6: Standard 1 (2008) Primary School

2-7: Standard 1 (2008) Primary School

Even though Jamila was still non verbal and could only utter single words like 'yes' and 'no', she was happy at school with the presence of a support teacher in the classroom. Her happiness was shown in her daily drawings featuring events at school with the teachers and students. She drew events that involved people in all her exercise books.

2.9: Drawings by Jamila showing events at school

2-13: Drawings by Jamila showing events at school

When she was seven, I met a long-lost friend who did craniosacral massage therapy. The therapy is a full-body treatment, with much emphasis on the head, neck, and shoulder regions. It improves the movement of the fluids in the spinal cord and brain. It also improves blood movement and helps cells in the brain get the nutrients necessary for normal functioning. It helps to flush out waste and toxins from the brain cells so the overactive or underactive parts of the brain are normalised. This therapy uses primary respiration and therapeutic touch to regulate the flow of cerebrospinal fluid. The effectiveness of this method complements the natural healing processes of the body, as it can easily bolster resistance to diseases and shows positive effects for a great range of medical problems associated with dysfunction and pain. When the body is healthy, the mind is healthy. I diligently sent Jamila for the massage therapy on a weekly basis for several months.

I first met Jamila back in 2009 in my therapy room. Back then, she was a 'frightened fearful child', but somehow we managed to build a trusting bond between us. From then on, I witnessed how she came out of her fear around people and social surroundings. She grows with confidence; though still shy, she knows what she wants and works towards it. Her weakness becomes her 'gift', and she is now sharing the pure rhythm of life with the world.

—Sum Mooi Soo

2-14: Sum Mooi Soo (Renew Earth-life Therapy Centre)

Along the way, Jamila was sent to several therapy centres to overcome her lack of literacy skills. When she started to speak short words and respond to questions at the age of eight, we decided to send her to a dyslexic centre for further help. It was a surprise when Jamila learned to read using phonic techniques taught by her aunt Noor Sa'adah Mohd Noordin, a dyslexia specialist.

2-15: Noor Sa'adah Mohd. Noordin. (Dyslexia Specialist)

It has been my utmost pleasure to have been given the opportunity to work with my beautiful talented niece Wan Jamila in her early years in 2010, struggling to overcome her literacy skills. As a specialist in dyslexia, the task given was quite a challenge indeed for me, as being autistic, she learns differently. Despite the difficulties and challenges, my special affection goes to Jamila for her hard work and perseverance, thriving her best when challenged. Her sense of curiosity and her ability to see the world in her unique perspective is indeed her source of creativity and brilliance! *'One doesn't have to be perfect to achieve big dreams.'* Keep soaring high, my dear; the sky is the limit.

—Noor Sa'adah Mohd Noordin

When I taught Jamila to use the protractor to draw circles, she transformed them into three-dimensional drawings, complete with shadings. This discovery told me she sees things in three dimensions. It helped me understand her more. Whenever she looks at a two-dimensional square figure, her mind visualises it as a three-dimensional form. At this milestone, I successfully managed to truly understand her. Jamila is a visual thinker, not a language-based thinker. She holds information in ways people can hardly understand. She sees things in ways others might find unimaginable. Certain parts of her brain function more than other parts.

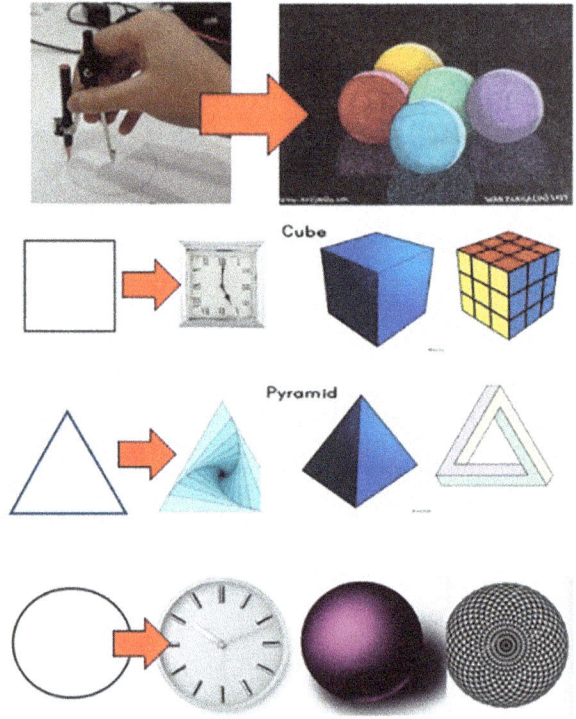

2-16: Jamila see things in 3-dimensional formv

At this juncture, Jamila became a much happier child when we understood each other better, and I feel more at ease in helping and guiding her.

2-17: Jamila at primary school

2-19: Jamila at primary school

2-21: Jamila at primary school

Since Jamila is a visual thinker, I had to break from the standard mould of teaching. I learned to adapt to her, not lead her. Once she was able to read, I started daily classes with her and her sister at home in a cosy study environment.

If they can't learn the way we teach, we teach the way they learn.

—Dr O. Ivar Lovaas

2-23: Compilation of express notes from book store (Mathematic)

2-24: Compilation of express notes from book store (Science)

2-25: Compilation of my research into lecture notes.

2-27: Study room at home.

2-28: Study room at home.

2-32: Study room at home.

2-33: My office room at architectural firm.

2-34: Kids' study room attached to Principal's office.

2-35: Kids' tuition room attached to Principal's room

In December 2010, I and another parent with a child who had special needs conducted a revision class program at the school during the school holidays to mentally prepare the children for the upcoming school session.

2-36: Class revision at school during December school holiday (2010)

2-37: Class revision at school during December school holiday (2010)

The standard school curriculum for mathematics offers multiple topics in one session. Jamila was good with focussing on a specific task, but she could not multitask. Therefore, the format in the government curriculum was not suitable for her. After several attempts at making her understand a topic, I discovered that a modular system was more applicable to her.

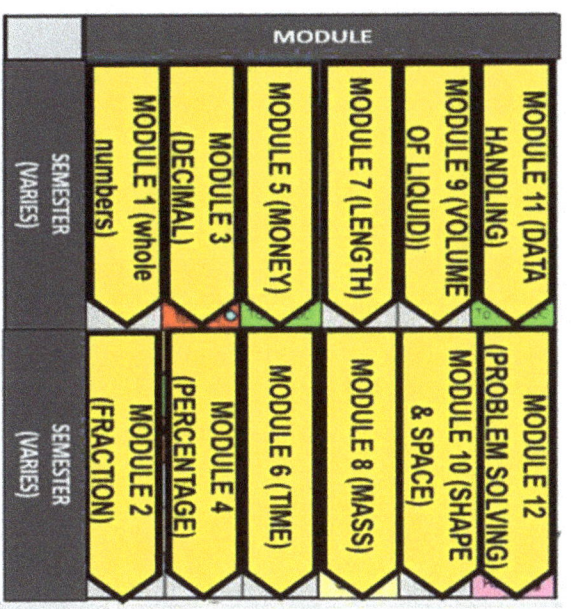

2-38: The standard government's school curriculum structure for mathematics in primary school with specific time frame for each section

2-39: Modular system curriculum structure for mathematics without limitation of time for each module.

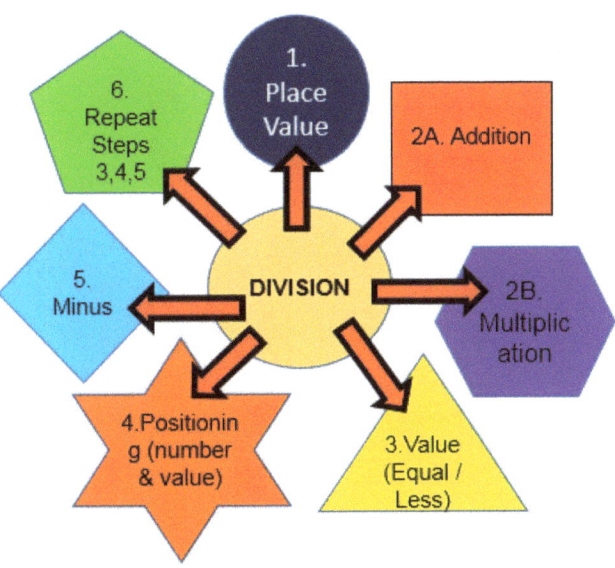

2-40: The modular system for mathematics (Division)

2-41: Teaching using conventional method by writing on the board.

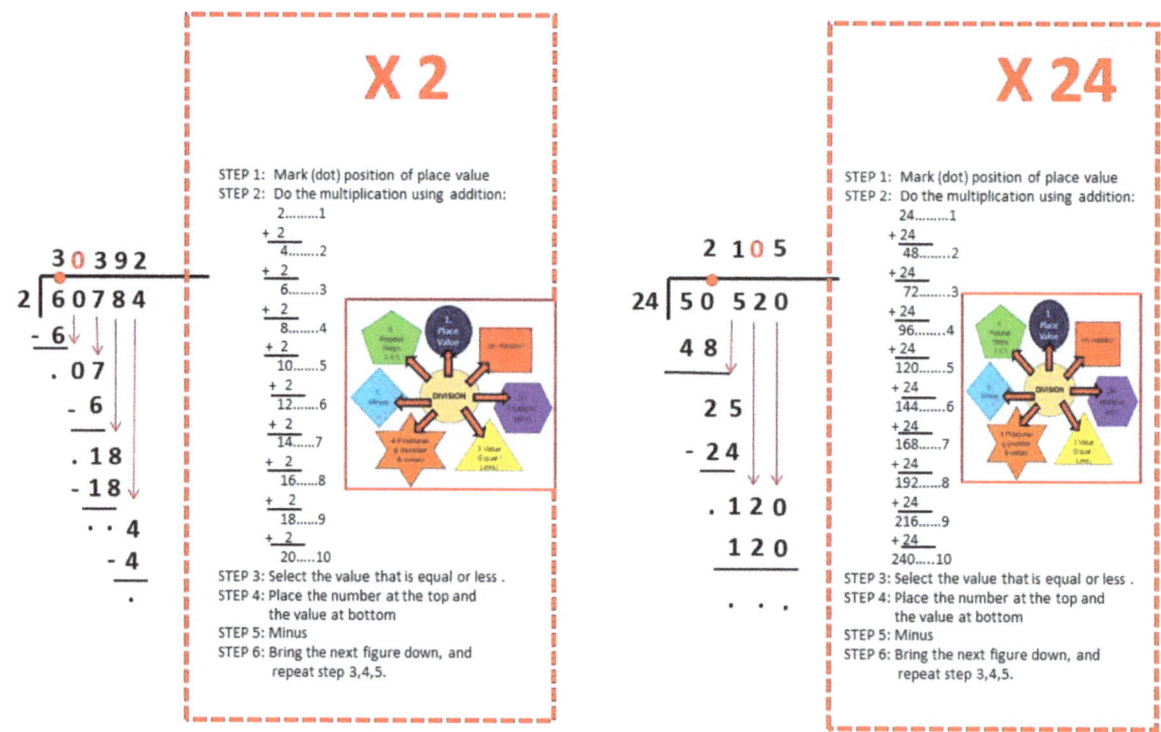

2-42: Teaching using technology by using software (power point and LCD projector to provide variety of delivery system and excitement in learning)

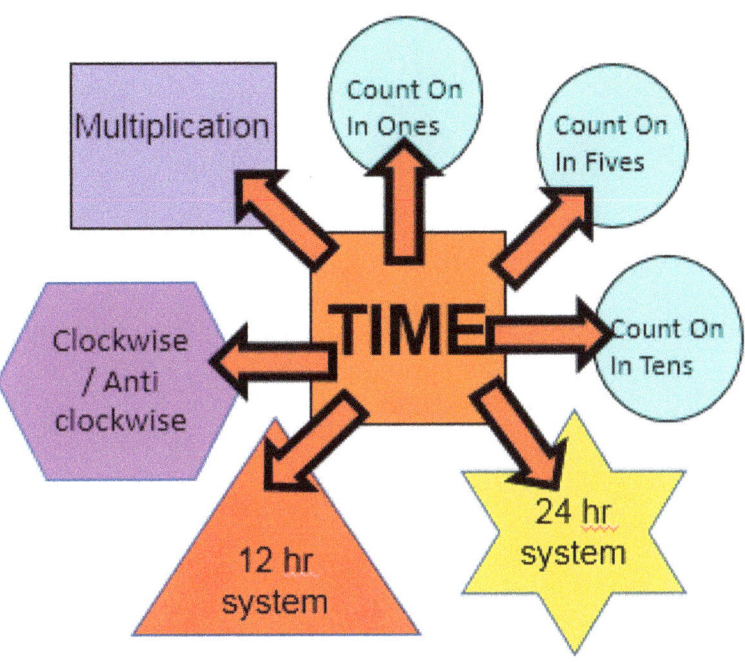

2-43: The modular system for mathematics (time)

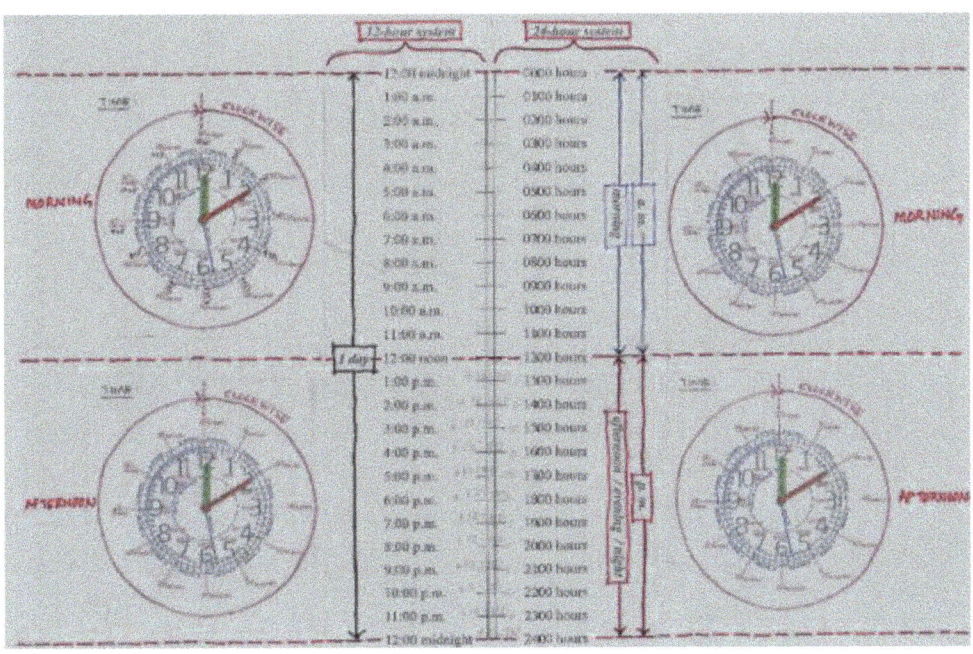

2-44: Teaching using a conventional method by writing on paper.

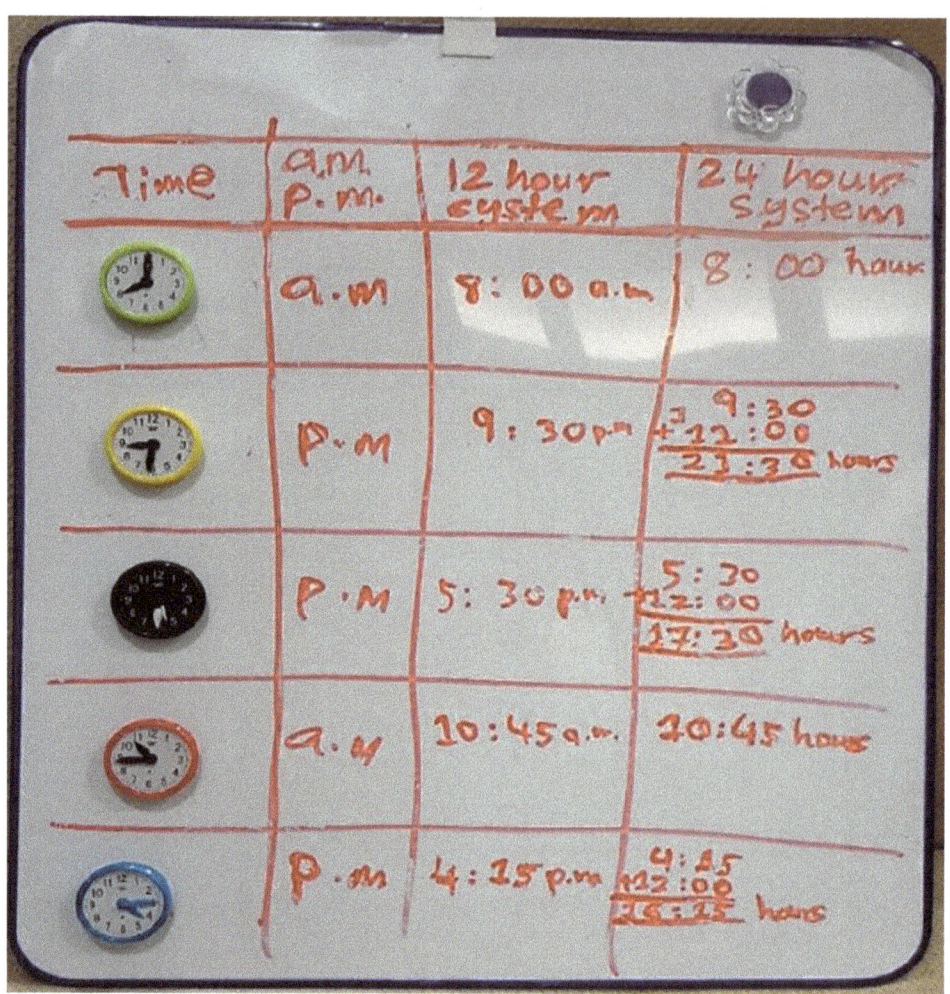

2-45: An interactive teaching method on a movable white board with miniature clocks

2-46: Mind mapping method for science subject.　　　2-47: Mind mapping method for science subject.

2-48: Modelling of farm animals for science subject for science subject.

2-49: Experiment for science subject.

2-50: Teaching process of painting for art lesson (2012)

2-51: Crayon technique 2012 painted by Jamila)

2-52: Watercolour technique (2012 painted by Jamila)

Jamila was not happy during standard 4 in 2012. She was all alone in her class without a support teacher and bullied by her classmates. She hardly learned anything because she ran out of the class every time it was time to learn. She managed to overcome her frustrations with the use of a digital software program she installed herself. She used her forefinger to draw and has produced thousands of digital drawings using this technique.

2-53: Jamila with her tablet doing digital drawing (2012)

2-56: Digital drawing (2012)

The year 2013 was another milestone. I needed to re-enrol her in standard 4. I requested the school principal assign her to the first class of standard 4 to be with Jemima. All the students in this class were very studious. And Jemima, who was a school prefect, protected and cared for her sister in the school. Jamila was happy in this new class with all her understanding classmates. Sketches in her exercise books reflected her happiness. She drew her schoolmates with all the multiracial people in different colours. At the school, she also showed her ability to dance. She could perform a complex dance after observing a specific dance movement briefly. She could also translate all the dance steps into drawings. She enjoyed dancing at the school concert and was very good at it. She danced gracefully and beautifully and was even able to memorise all the dance steps.

A rather timid-appearing little girl clutching her mother's hand and walking through the gates of Sekolah Sri Acmar in the year 2009 soon became the talk of the school. Her extraordinary talents in drawing and dancing were tremendous. She used to score A for her art and multi praises from the audience who watched her dancing. Although diagnosed with autism, she managed to score a C for her science in the UPSR examination. She also captured the hearts of the other schoolmates and teachers. Having taught her makes me feel proud of her achievements. The fruit of the labour of the teachers in Sekolah Sri Acmar shines like a star, and she is non other than Wan Jamila.

—Miss Judith Anthony

2-57: Miss Judith Anthony vice principal Sri Acmar Primary School

2-58: Jamila is second from right and Jemima is third from right (2013)

2-59: Jamila is at the center (2013)

2-60: Drawings by Jamila in her school exercise book. She named her classmates as "The Team Rainbow Dash" (2013)

2-61: Drawing by Jamila, titled "People of Malaysia". The colorful people reflect her multi-racial friends at the school (2013)

2-64: Jamila's drawing of all the dance activities of school concert from her memory (2013)

2-65: School concert. Jamila at far right (2013)

My Journey with Artjamila

2-66: School concert. Jamila at far right (2013)

2-67: Jamila (far left, front line) with schoolmates during UPSR examination briefing by the school's principal (2015)

The years 2012 and 2013 were not good years for me due to multiple problems, stress related to family matters, and a high volume of work commitment. I could not achieve my goal to fully concentrate on Jamila's education and help her prepare herself for the government elementary examination (UPSR) in 2013. Jamila had to perform on her own. And I am glad she managed to score a C on the science part of the exam.

Chapter 3
HOMESCHOOL: ART AS THERAPY

In 2016, I moved Jamila to the government secondary school under the special needs program with an intention of entering her into the inclusive program. This would enable her to follow the normal school system and to enter the higher level of education. Preparing myself was a tough challenge, but eventually I decided to retire in December 2015 from all my careers and fully concentrate on her. It was a very difficult decision for me to make, as I was at the pinnacle of success in my career. I had achieved everything I wanted to achieve in my profession. But I realised that I could not rewind the clock if I were to miss the golden opportunity to help Jamila in her secondary education.

Unfortunately, I was ill throughout 2015 and 2016. In August 2016, I was diagnosed with colon cancer. The series of major operations and medical treatments that followed were intensive. Unfortunately, I could not monitor her education in the secondary school.

After my recovery in the first part of 2017, Jamila started to lose interest in school, due to the academic level in the special needs program being too low for her. When I referred to the curriculum in the mainstream program, I realised that the academic level with the new system was too high for Jamila. I arrived at a dead end at that point.

The only solution was homeschool. I decided to take charge. I would observe my daughter and derive my own customised workable solutions for my unique daughter. Thus, I developed a learning system that is people-centred (humanistic pedagogy, focussing on the emotional and social development of children as part of achieving success, as opposed to the structured system in the school curriculum). It is a system applied by the Montessori program. I decided to concentrate on what my daughter can do (her strengths, rather than on what she cannot do).

Start with what is right rather than what is acceptable.

—Franz Kafka

The desire must come from the child, not us.

—Ruth

I was inspired by Stephen Wiltshire MBE, who is a British architectural artist and autistic savant. He is known for his ability to draw from memory a landscape after seeing it just once. Similarly, Jamila draws the events from school when she gets home. Jamila has the ability to draw from her memory.

3-1: Sketches of the dance steps drawn from Jamila's memory when she reached home from school (2013)

3-2: Sketches of the dance drawn from Jamila's memory when she reached home from school concert (2013)

At this milestone, I decided to train her in proper drawing techniques and seek advice from several local artists to evaluate her talent. The positive remarks from them gave me the strength to move forward with her art. My curriculum was designed with "art as a therapy" at its core. I managed to have a deeper connection with my daughter, taking a holistic approach. The fruit of my labour shone like a star when she became an artist at the age of fourteen in 2016. My daughter might have achieved developmental and societal behaviour milestones in a different order from her peers, but she is able to accomplish her own victories. One doesn't have to be perfect to achieve big dreams. My child's weakness became a gift, and my daughter is now sharing the pureness of the rhythm of life with the world.

I was hesitant to let go of my profession at first, but now I'm glad to have done so. Seeing how I stand now, I'm doing better with my daughter than I was before. And with that, I feel fulfilled. The hardest decision I made was to leave my profession as an associate professor and principal to my own architectural practice, but it was also the best decision I made. Working as an associate professor and practising as an architect served only for my own self-satisfaction. Being an art manager to my own daughter is more fulfilling. The notion that she has a profession as an artist is most satisfying. In turn, she contributes to the society of autism and the public at large through charity exhibitions and sharing sessions.

I am glad that my thirty years of passion in architecture and academics can be applied to this new profession of mine as an art manager. My knowledge as a lecturer enabled me to teach my daughters. And my experience as an academician and former head of an architectural program in the university helped me to design my own homeschool program for my daughter. I apply my knowledge in running my architectural firm to my new profession as art manager managing Artjamila. It is a wonderful experience.

3-3: Jamila doing mural painting (2017)

3-4: Jamila in her art studio (2017)

3-5: Jamila in her art studio (2016)

3-6: Jamila in her art studio (2018)

As opposed to the normal education system ("bottom up"), my approach is "top to bottom". I identify Jamila's strength and create her profession. Then I structure a curriculum to match her profession. The approach is tailored towards practical application. Each practical subject (art, home science, exercise, exhibitions, and tours) has a component of all the subjects oriented in secondary school, like mathematics, science, English, Malay language, and history/geography.

All the practical subjects are included with occupational and speech therapy.

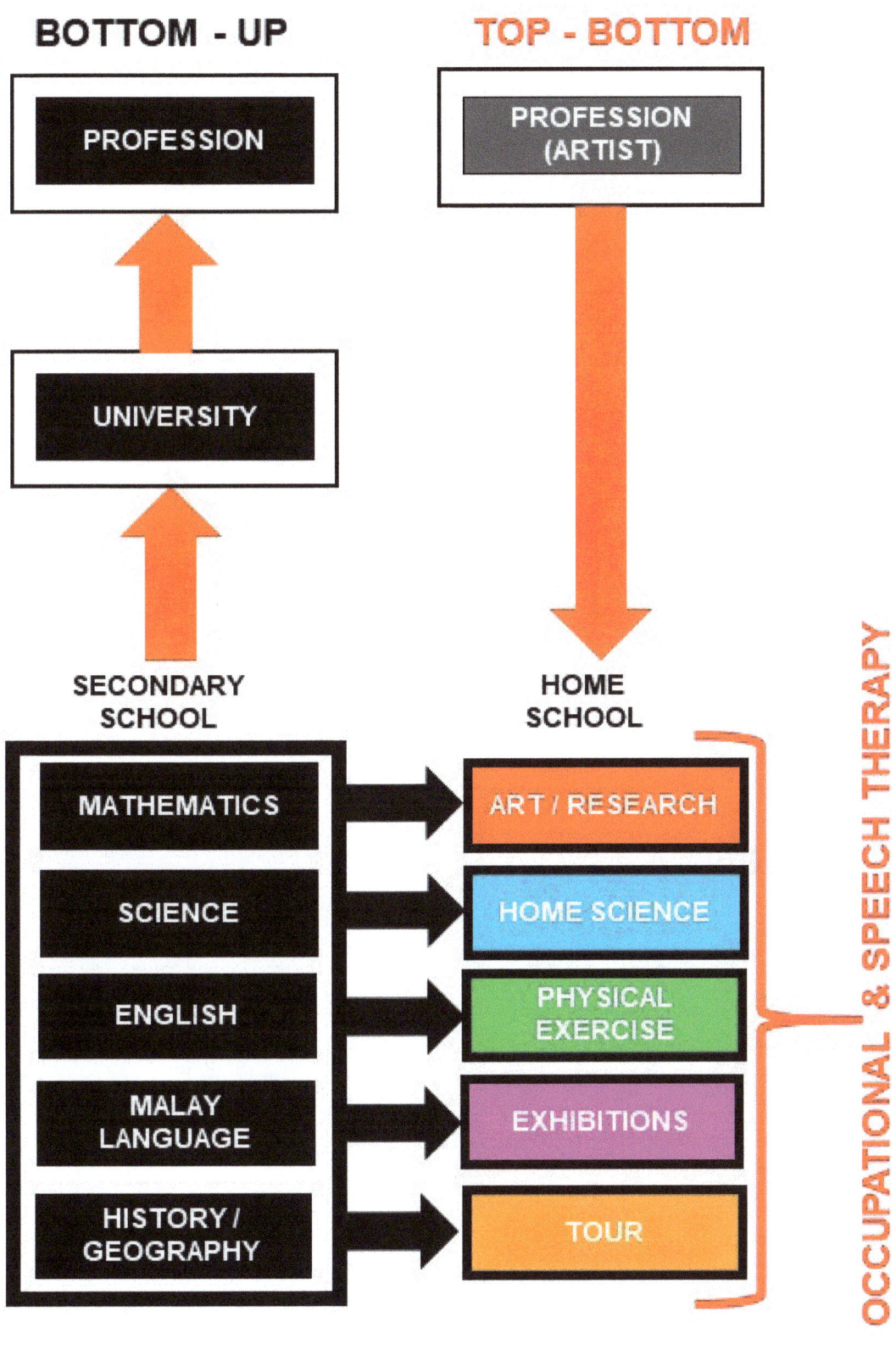

3-7: Educational Approach

There are so many options of routes to take towards getting to a destination. The options for Jamila are as follows:

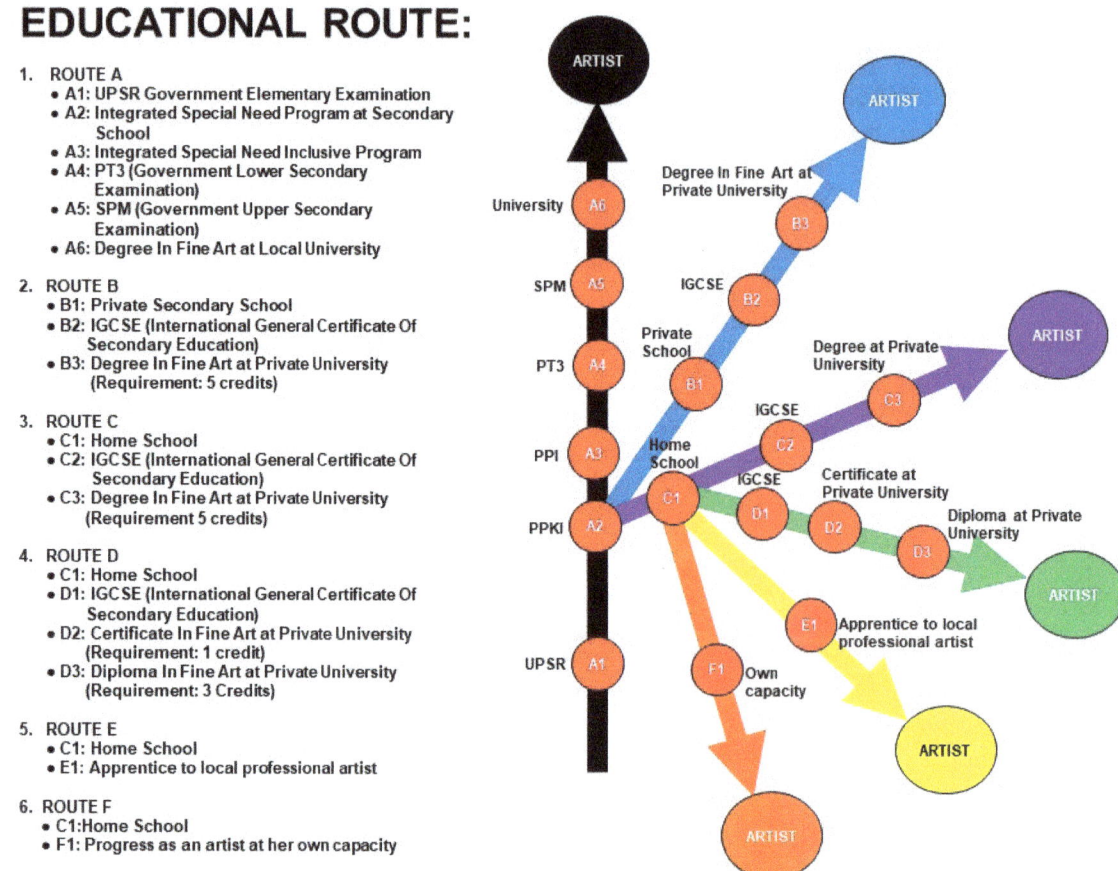

EDUCATIONAL ROUTE:

1. ROUTE A
   - A1: UPSR Government Elementary Examination
   - A2: Integrated Special Need Program at Secondary School
   - A3: Integrated Special Need Inclusive Program
   - A4: PT3 (Government Lower Secondary Examination)
   - A5: SPM (Government Upper Secondary Examination)
   - A6: Degree In Fine Art at Local University

2. ROUTE B
   - B1: Private Secondary School
   - B2: IGCSE (International General Certificate Of Secondary Education)
   - B3: Degree In Fine Art at Private University (Requirement: 5 credits)

3. ROUTE C
   - C1: Home School
   - C2: IGCSE (International General Certificate Of Secondary Education)
   - C3: Degree In Fine Art at Private University (Requirement 5 credits)

4. ROUTE D
   - C1: Home School
   - D1: IGCSE (International General Certificate Of Secondary Education)
   - D2: Certificate In Fine Art at Private University (Requirement: 1 credit)
   - D3: Diploma In Fine Art at Private University (Requirement: 3 Credits)

5. ROUTE E
   - C1: Home School
   - E1: Apprentice to local professional artist

6. ROUTE F
   - C1: Home School
   - F1: Progress as an artist at her own capacity

3-8: Educational Route

Note:

1. Route A is not suitable for Jamila because the curriculum at PPKI is tailored towards the lowest standard of the special children in the school. As such it is not suitable for Jamila, since Jamila sat for UPSR and scored a C for Science. In addition, the curriculum for PT3 and SPM is too high a standard, and the national language and history are even mandatory subjects to pass. Therefore, it is not suitable for most autistic students, as their weakness is very commonly national language and composition.
2. Route B is more suitable for autistic students. Unfortunately, it is not suitable for Jamila.
3. Route C is achievable. The requirement for entry to a degree in fine art programme is 5 credits. Unfortunately, this is not a target for Jamila because 80 per cent of Jamila's current curriculum structure is art.
4. Route D is also achievable, it is an option to Jamila.
5. Route E is achievable. Currently, Jamila is getting guidance from several professional artists in the country.
6. Route F is achievable. Currently, Jamila is travelling as an artist at her own capacity.

My Journey with Artjamila

The homeschool curriculum structure designed for Jamila is found in item 3.9 below. Each of the sections is to be read with the activities listed on the following pages.

1. Social skills (activities 1 to 26)
2. Home science (activities 27 to 30h)
3. Art as profession (graph 3C and activities 31 and 32)

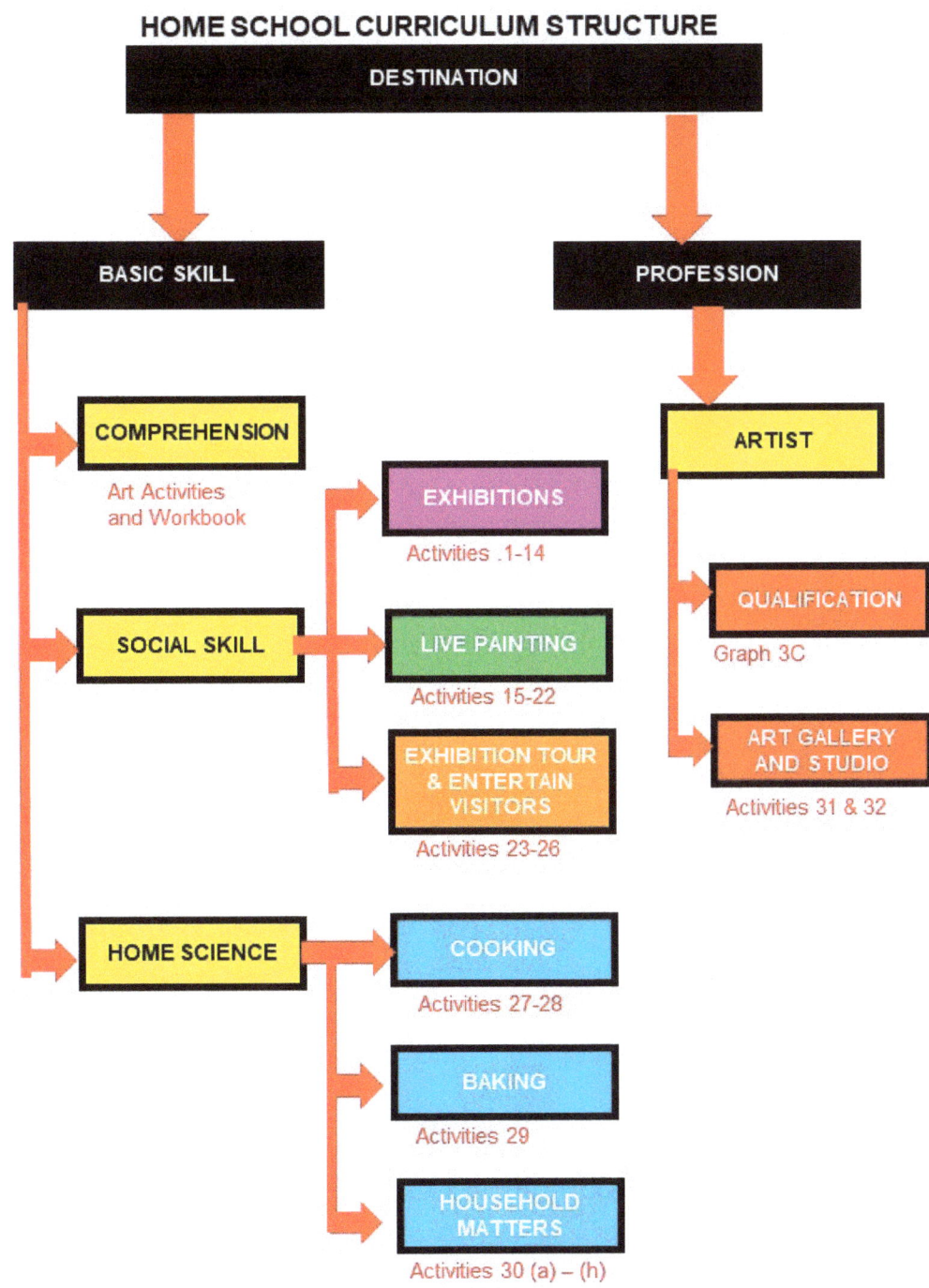

3-9: Home School Curriculum Structure

The activities required for her to participate have helped Jamila to improve her social skills. She is required to attend exhibitions, perform live drawings, and socialise with art lovers and the public.

3-11: Group Exhibition (IACON)

ACTIVITY 1: Group Exhibition: Independent Arts, Converge & Connect (IACON) at TM Convention Centre, Kuala Lumpur, Malaysia from 18 to 19th March 2017

3-13: Group Exhibition (Avenue K)

ACTIVITY 2: Group Charity Exhibition: Art & Craft Exhibition at Avenue K, Kuala Lumpur, Malaysia from 24th March 2017 to 7th April 2017

3-15: Group Exhibition (The Ledge Gallery)

ACTIVITY 3: Group Charity Exhibition: Art & Craft Exhibition at The Ledge Art Gallery, One Utama, Kuala Lumpur, Malaysia from 1st April 2017 to 30th April 2017

3-16: Solo exhibition (Concorde Hotel Shah Alam, Selangor, Malaysia)

ACTIVITY 4: Solo Exhibition at Concorde Hotel Shah Alam, Selangor, Malaysia on 21st April 2017.

3-17: His Royal Highness, Tengku Amir Shah (the crown prince of Selangor visited Jamila's exhibition and signed Jamila's painting).

ACTIVITY 5: Group Exhibition at Malaysian Institute of Architects (PAM, Kuala Lumpur, Malaysia on 25th April 2017)

3-18: Group Exhibition at PAM.

3-20: Group Exhibition (The Ledge Gallery)

ACTIVITY 6: Group Exhibition: Art & Craft Exhibition at The Ledge Art Gallery, One Utama, Kuala Lumpur, Malaysia from July, August and September 2017.

3-23: Critique session at Shah Alam Art Gallery

ACTIVITY 7: Critique Session at Shah Alam Art Gallery, Selangor, Malaysia.

3-24: Group Exhibition at International Forum

ACTIVITY 8: Exhibition at International Montessori Forum 19-20th August 2017 at Kuala Lumpur, Malaysia.

My Journey with Artjamila

3-26: Art Bazaar at Bank Negara Malaysia

ACTIVITY 9: Art Bazaar 22-28 November 2017 at Museum & Art Gallery, Bank Negara Malaysia

3-35: Imago Mundi 3 Nation

ACTIVITY 10: Imago Mundi 3 Nation (Malaysia, Singapore, Indonesia Exhibition from 5 to 30 January 2018 at Hulo Hotel & Art Gallery, Kuala Lumpur, Malaysia)

3-38: ArtEDecor, Matrade, KL, Malaysia

ACTIVITY 11: Art & Décor (ArtEDecor) Exhibition from 8-11th March 2018 at Matrade Exhibition & Convention Centre, Kuala Lumpur, Malaysia.

3-39: ArtEDecor, Matrade, KL, Malaysia

ACTIVITY 12: Exhibition by National Autism Centre (NASOM) 19-21 April 2018 at Utropolis Event Centre, Selangor, Malaysia.

3-45: NASOM exhibition. Formal visit by Her Majesty Tengku Permaisuri Norashikin, the queen of Selangor (second from left)

My Journey with Artjamila

3-52: Live drawing at TV Station TV9, KL Malaysia

ACTIVITY 14: Live Drawing at television Station TV9, Malaysia on 26th Mac 2017

3-54: Live painting at TV Station TV1, KL Malaysia

ACTIVITY 15: Live painting on air at television station, TV1 on 11 July 2017 at an event called "Merdeka Painting", Kuala Lumpur, Malaysia.

3-55: Live mural painting at SMK Seksyen 9, Shah Alam, Selangor, Malaysia

ACTIVITY 16: Live Painting at secondary school (SMK Seksyen 9, Shah Alam, Selangor, Malaysia from 7 to 13 May 2017; theme "Underwater World: Mermaids")

3-56: Live mural painting at SMK Seksyen 9, Shah Alam, Selangor, Malaysia

3-58: Live drawing in a sharing session seminar at Manipal Hospital, Selangor, Malaysia

ACTIVITY 17: Live drawing during seminar titled "Empowering Autism: Understand, Accept, and Love" on 27 May 2017 at Manipal Hospital Klang, Selangor, Malaysia

3-59: Live painting "Malaysia Makes History" Event.

ACTIVITY 18: Live painting on 4 August 2017 at an event titled "Malaysia Makes History" at MAEPS Serdang, Selangor

3-62: Live painting at SMK Danau Kota, KL, Malaysia

ACTIVITY 19: Live painting on 8 August 2017 at an event in a school in SMK Danau Kota, Kuala Lumpur, Malaysia

My Journey with Artjamila

ACTIVITY 20: Live painting on 14 August 2017 at an event titled "Merdeka Live Painting" in One Utama Shopping Complex, Kuala Lumpur, Malaysia

3-64: Merdeka live painting officiated by Deputy Minister Tourism Malaysia

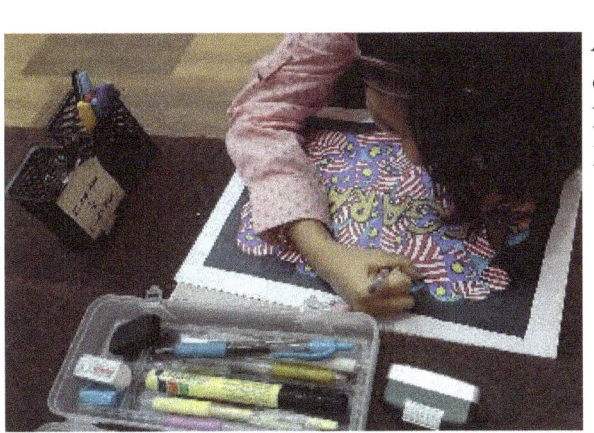

ACTIVITY 21: Live painting competition on 29 July 2017 at the National Art Gallery, Kuala Lumpur, Malaysia

3-70: Live painting competition at National Art Gallery, KL, Malaysia

3-68: Live painting competition

ACTIVITY 22: Press conference with local newspaper (Kosmo on 14 August 2017)

3-71: Press conference with Kosmo newspaper

ACTIVITY 23: Press conference with a group of reporters from Malaysian and Indonesian newspapers and magazines on 17 August 2017 on an event called "Craft from the Heart" organised by Selangor State Economic Planning Unit (UPEN)

3-73: Press conference with group of reporters from Malaysian and Indonesian newspapers and magazines organized by Selangor State Economic Planning Unit (UPEN)

ACTIVITY 24: Tour to exhibitions by others.

3-77: Tour to exhibitions by others

3-85: Entertain visitors at gallery

ACTIVITY 25: Entertain visitors at artjamila gallery

3-88: The art of cooking "Roti Jala"

3-90: The art of cooking "Roti Jala"

ACTIVITY 26: Cooking ("Roti Jala": The art of netting on hot plate)

3-91: The art of cooking "Roti Jala"

3-92: The art of cooking "Roti Jala"

3-95: The art of cooking. Preparation onions

3-96: The art of cooking. Frying onions

ACTIVITY 27: Preparation and Frying of onions.

ACTIVITY 28: Baking Cup Cakes

3-97: Baking

3-98: Baking

3-99: Baking

3-100: Baking

3-101: Baking

ACTIVITY 29: Household matters (Vocational Training of Daily Activity)

3-103: Organize kitchen utensils

3-104: Organize kitchen utensils

3-105: Organize kitchen utensils

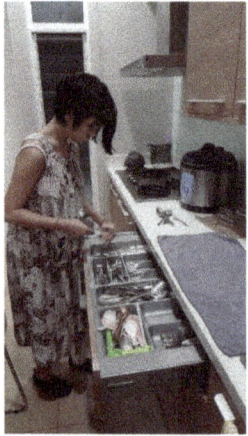
3-106: Organize kitchen utensils

3-107: Organize kitchen utensils

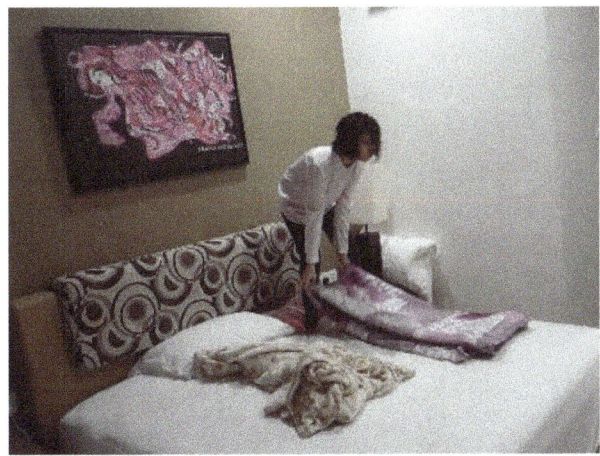
3-109: Organize mattress

ACTIVITY 30: Household matters
(Vocational Training of Daily Activity)

3-112: Open all doors and windows

ACTIVITY 31: Household matters
(Vocational Training of Daily Activity)

 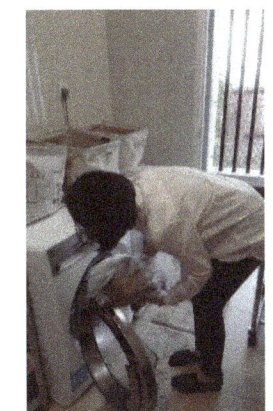
3-115: Laundry routine   3-117: Laundry routine

ACTIVITY 32: Household matters
(Vocational Training of Daily Activity)

3-123: Laundry   3-126: Laundry

ACTIVITY 33: Household matters
(Vocational Training of Daily Activity)

ACTIVITY 34: Household matters (Vocational Training of Daily Activity)

3-127: Prepare breakfast

3-128: Prepare breakfast

3-130: Prepare breakfast

3-133: Wash dishes

ACTIVITY 35: Daily painting activity in art studio

3-135: Daily painting activity in art studio

Art encourages fine motor skills, neural development, and problem-solving abilities. I saw a big improvement in Jamila's capability with art therapy. She has reduced her autistic characteristics and improved on the following aspects:

Behavioural
- She reduced her unusual behaviour in responding to her surroundings.
- She can cope with a variety of situations.
- Her sensitivity to sound and texture has decreased.
- She improved her attention span for a longer period of time. In fact, she can focus for a long duration.
- She is able to change her routines, such as doing things in the same order every time.

Social interaction
- She is able to respond to non-verbal forms of communication that many of us take for granted, like facial expressions, physical gestures, and eye contact.
- Now Jamila can understand and express her needs.
- She is also able to interpret and understand the needs of others.
- She enjoys having friends and no longer appears distant and aloof.
- She like to share enjoyment, interests, and activities with other people.
- She has improved her social and emotional responsiveness. Jamila enjoys socialising with guests who visit her gallery and the people at the exhibitions.

Communication
- She has improved her communication, especially with me and the family members and often uses language in a limited way.
- She increased her number of words in a sentence, especially related to her tasks and to her needs. But she only speaks about topics that are of interest to her, which makes the give and take in communication difficult.
- She can request what she desires verbally.

Understanding and comprehending
- She can take instructions and understand them.
- She can make decisions on the techniques of drawing and choice of colours she wants to create for each painting.
- She is able to make decisions on other matters as well.
- She is able to understand explanations on the rationality of a situation.

Responsibility
- She can self-program herself to perform her tasks and to complete her work according to the times and schedules given in a calendar format.
- She is responsible for her work.
- She can perform her tasks without prompting.

The art activities are a very positive method of healing for Jamila. Jamila uses art to make her soul be heard. She explores her intuitive (third eye) ability during her art creation. She learns to use her intuition, versus merely following her thoughts. Her intuition guides her with the type of stroke and the speed of the brush her soul desires. This combat and struggle between intuition and thought carries over into her daily tasks, relationships, and self-love. Her intuition and happiness grow stronger in this process.

Jamila is able to focus for a long duration of time whenever she is in the act of creating art. Art is a meditation for her. Her hands and brain are focused on a non-stressful activity just long enough to allow her to drift off into a meditative state. In general, Jamila is a happier person ever since she has indulged in art. The activity of creating art brings calmness, and calmness leads to happiness. Art is ultimately a therapeutic medium, just like music.

In 2017 I started to share my journey with the general public by giving my experiences and techniques in teaching and guiding Jamila through the journey. I showed the journey in a step-by-step format and highlight all the important milestones of decision making, sacrifices and changes of route and directions we went through. I also highlighted the many options towards getting to a destination.

1. Sharing session with the public at Manipal Hospital in Klang, Selangor, Malaysia on 27 May 2017.

3-144: Brochure sharing session at Manipal Hospital

3-145: Sharing session at Manipal Hospital

3-146: Sharing session at Manipal Hospital

2. Sharing session with a Secondary School (Parents & Teachers) at SMK Danau Kota, Kuala Lumpur, Malaysia on 8 August 2017.

3-149: Sharing session at SMK Danau Kota, KL, Malaysia

3-150: Sharing session at SMK Danau Kota, KL, Malaysia

3. Sharing session with the general public at International Montessori Forum 2017 Malaysia on 19 August 2018 at Kuala Lumpur, Malaysia.

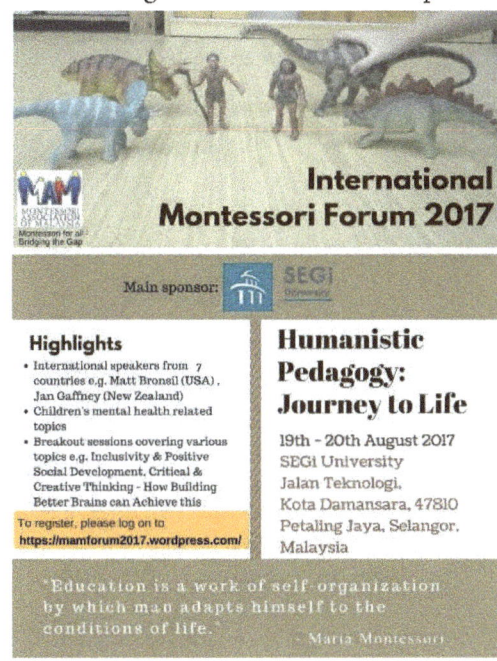

3-152: Sharing session at International Montessori Forum

3-151: Sharing session at International Montessori Forum

3-153: Sharing session at International Montessori Forum

4. Sharing session with the public at Manipal Hospital in Klang, Selangor, Malaysia on 11 November 2017.

3-154: Sharing session at Manipal Hospital

3-155: Sharing session at Manipal Hospital

3-156: Sharing session at Manipal Hospital

5. Sharing session with staff of Securities Commission (SC) Malaysia on 26th April 2018 at SC Headquarters, Kuala Lumpur, Malaysia.

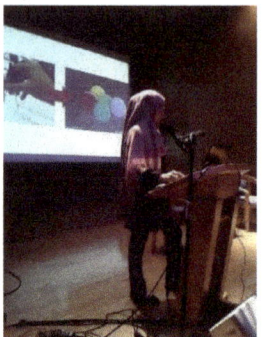

3-157: Sharing session at Securities Commission Malaysia

3-158: Sharing session at SC Malaysia

The fifteen years of my journey from June 2002 to May 2018 was a journey full of discovery. As a mother, I am satisfied with Jamila's achievement in this Part 1 Journey. My journey continues. I need to move forward with more improvement and achievement with my daughter, especially her ability to survive on her own and be independent. My Part 2 objectives are:

1. To improve her language development
2. To improve her difficulties in initiating and sustaining conversations
3. To improve her vocabulary
4. To prepare her with actions to take during an emergency.
5. To make her independent with handling money.
6. To uplift further her achievement as an artist.
7. And many more.

I am exploring more techniques and adventure with Artjamila and am currently doing some adjustments to her daily schedule to insert other activities like religious studies and basic survival skills. I will start to embark in artificial intelligence software to improve her cognitive ability and improve the content of her curriculum with a more structured timetable. The discoveries of this adventure will be documented in my "Part 2" journey with Artjamila.

Chapter 4

TURNING MEMORIES INTO MASTERPIECES

Jamila puts her memories into masterpieces. Her drawings can be divided into three major categories.

1. Her emotions
    a. Happiness
    b. Sadness
    c. Calm
    d. Restless

5. What she likes
    a. Travelling with Malaysian Airlines
    b. Beauty (Princess and women with long hair like Rapunzel from Disney)
    c. Cooking and baking / teapots
    d. Fashion and modelling
    e. Dancing
    f. Flowers

7. Events she experienced
    a. Travelling and weekend outings with her mother and her younger sister (*Three Ladies*)
    b. Dance concert at primary school
    c. Multi-racial people at the primary school
    d. Group photo during group tour
    e. Visits to aquarium
    f. Yearly class party at primary school
    g. Schoolmates
    h. Family activities

Most of Jamila's recent painting work relates to her early years of drawings.

E2: CALM (A portrait that resembles Jamila's character as "grace").

4-1: Early years digital drawing (*Beautiful Women, Series B45*) 2015

4-2: Recent work (*Anora, Series 1B*) 2016

L2: Beauty (drawings inspired by women with long hair like Disney's Rapunzel)

4-3: Early years digital drawing (*Beautiful Women, Series B12*) 2012

4-4: Recent work (*Rapunzel, Series 5B*) 2017

L3: Teapots (teapots represent Jamila's passion for cooking)

4-5: Early years digital drawing (*Family Activities, Series FA28*) 2013

4-6: Recent work (*Teapots, Series 7 "The Pleasant Taste of Tea*) 2018

L4: Fashion and modelling (Jamila is passionate about fashion and modelling).

4-7: Early years digital drawing (*Fashion and modelling, Series F14*) 2013

4-8: Recent work (*Kebaya Girls, Series 1*) 2016

L5: Dancing (Jamila loves to dance)

4-9: Early years sketches on art paper (*Dance Consert, Series D11*) 2013

4-10: Recent work (*Malay Traditional Dance, Zapin, Series 2*) 2016

L6: Flowers (Jamila likes to draw flowers she imagines in her garden).

4-11: Early years digital drawing (*Flowers, Series 1*) 2012

4-12: Recent work (*Orchids Flowers, Series 1*) 2018

M1: Events she experienced (Most of her travels during her childhood were with her mother and her younger sister. *Three Ladies* was inspired by those memories).

4-13B: Early years digital drawing (*Three Ladies, Series TL44*) 2012

4-14: Recent work (*Three Ladies in Kebaya, Series 2B*) 2017

M3: Events she experienced (multiracial people at her primary school)

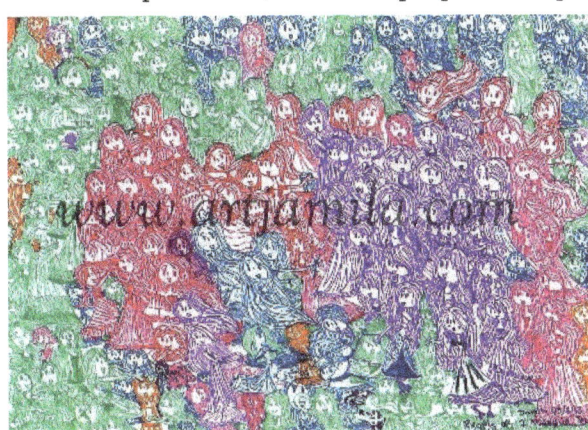 

4-15: Early years sketches on art paper (*Multiracial People, Series S1*) 2013

4-16: Recent work (*Schoolmates, Series 2*) 2016

M4: Events she experienced (group photo taken during her travels)

4-17: Early years sketches on notepad (*Group Photo During Group Tour, Series GT1*) 2012

4-18: Recent work (*Group Photo during Her Travels, Series 1*) 2016

M5: EVENTS SHE EXPERIENCED (Memories of visit to an aquarium)

4-19B: Early years digital drawing (*Visit to Aquaria, Series FM2*) 2012

4-20: Recent work (*Fish Mosaic, Series 10, the Art of Togetherness*) 2017

4-21B: Early years digital drawing (*Visit to aquarium, Series FM1,Mermaid*) 2012

4-22: Recent work (*Mermaids, Series 2, Life Beyond Boundaries*) 2017

M7: Events she experienced (her precious memories with her schoolmates)

4-23: Early years digital drawing (*Schoolmates, Series SM39*) 2013

4-24: Recent work (*Schoolmates, Series 1*) 2016

M8: Events she experienced (her precious memories with her cats)

4-25: Early years digital drawing (*Family Activities, Series FA26, Cats in Basket*) 2013

4-26 Recent work (*Cats in Baskets, Series 2, The Art of Togetherness*) 2018

M9: Events she experienced (her precious memories with visit to butterfly park)

4-27: Early years digital drawing (*Butterflies, Series 1*) 2013

4-28: Recent work (*Butterflies, Series 1, Flying High*) 2018

M10: Events she experienced (her precious memories with her cat, Smokey)

4-29: Our beloved home cat (Photo of Smokey in bed) 2016

4-29B: Our beloved home cat (Photo of Smokey sleeping in her bed) 2016

4-30: Recent Work *(Cat in Pyjamas Series 1)* 2018

M11: Events she experienced (her precious memories of Independence Day celebration at primary school)

4-31: Photo of Independence Day Celebration at Primary School (Merdeka) 2013

4-31B: Photo of School Parade at Primary School, 2013

4-32: Early years sketches on paper *(Schoolmates, Series SM22, People of Malaysia)* 2013

4-33: Recent work *(Unity in Diversity, Series 2, Merdeka)* 2017

M12: Events she experienced (her precious memories of Independence Day celebration)

4-34: Photo of three major races in primary school (Malay, Chinese, Indian) 2013

4-34B: Photo of people of Malaysia carrying Malaysian flag, 2013

4-35: Recent Work: (*Malaysian Flag Series 1*) 2016

Chapter 5
ARTJAMILA'S BIOGRAPHY AND ACHIEVEMENTS:

"Masterpiece of Memories"

5-1 Jamila in art studio (2018)

Artist: Wan Jamila Wan Shaiful Bahri
Age: 15 in 2018
Studio Base: Shah Alam, Selangor, Malaysia.
Qualification: Home School
Fb page: @artjamilapage
Fb: Art Jamila
Ig: artjamila
Email: artjamila2002@gmail.com
Mobile: +6019-3152662

Social Media Links:
Fb page: https://www.facebook.com/artjamilapage.com
Fb: https://www.facebook.com.artjamila2002
Ig: https://www.Instagram.com/artjamila
Website: www.artjamila.com

Jamila started drawing as a tool for communication in 2006 (at age four), and now this gifted talent has paved her path, becoming an artist when she was only fourteen years old. At fifteen, she was invited to join a three nations exhibition, "Imago Mundi", featuring artists of Malaysia, Indonesia, and Singapore. The show brought her to a national level. Parallel to that, she was invited to join ArtEDecor in Matrade from 8 to 11 May 2018, which gave her further recognition as a national artist. Her journey as an artist flourished in less than a year.

5-2: Brochure Exhibition ArtEDecor at Malaysia Trade Center (Matrade). Picture of Artjamila at bottom left (2018)

Throughout her artistic journey until 30 March 2018, Jamila was featured in several magazines, including:
    a. Gaya Travel (2017), "Selangor's Passion Expressed through Crafts from the Heart".
    b. Iris (January 2018), "Young Artist with Big Talent".
    c. Star Media Group's Kuntum (April 2018), "The Magical Touch of Jamila".
    Institute of Language and Literature Malaysia (DBP) (April 2018), "Young Autistic Girl: A Shining Star in the Sky".

My Journey with Artjamila

5-3: Gaya Travel (2017), "Selangor's Passion Expressed through Crafts from the Heart".

5-4: Iris (January 2018), "Young Artist with Big Talent".

5-5: Star Media Group's, Kuntum (April 2018), "The Magical Touch of Jamila".

5-6: Institute of Language and Literature Malaysia (DBP) (April 2018), "Young Autistic Girl: A Shining Star in the Sky".

My Journey with Artjamila

She was broadcast drawing live on several television stations including:

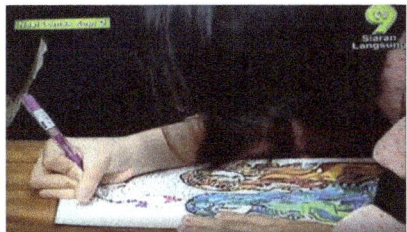  

5-7: 26 March 2017, TV9 Kopitiam (Live painting, *Three Ladies Series 5A*)

5-8: 11 July 2017, TV1 Selamat Pagi Malaysia (Live painting, *Unity in Diversity Series 1: Malaysian Flag*)

5-9: 7 April 2018, TV3, Borak Kopitiam (Painting, *Cats in Baskets*)

Her story was also broadcast through a documentary by TV3 on 5 January 2018. It spoke of Jamila only being a teenager of fourteen and how she has managed up till now as a rising artist. She holds an abundance of promising talent embedded in her, and her paintings catch the eyes of well-known art collectors. Her works, such as *Three Ladies* and *Fish Mosaic* symbolise the precious moments of her life. For example, the *Three Ladies* paintings are meant to speak of the close relationship shared between Jamila, me (her mother), and Jemima (her younger sister). The *Fish Mosaic* series captures the memory of a family outing in Kilim Geological Park in Langkawi, Malaysia. The journey of this child expands quickly, bringing the name of the country to the world.

5-10: 5 January 2018, TV3 Malaysia Hari Ini (a documentary by TV3)

5-11: 5 January 2018, TV3 Malaysia Hari Ini (a documentary by TV3)

Her journey was covered in the local newspapers, including:

- Kosmo Malaysia (3 April 2017), "Amateur Autistic Artist with Big Talent".
- Kosmo Malaysia (14 August 2017), "Wan Jamila's Empire of Art".
- Kosmo Malaysia (14 August 2017), "The Creation of Art for Independence Day".
- Malay Mail Malaysia (14 August 2017), "Merdeka Theme Brings out Best in Artists".
- Malay Mail Malaysia (20 September 2017), "Speaking through Art".

5-12: Kosmo Malaysia on 3 April 2017, "Amateur Autistic Artist with Big Talent".

5-13: Kosmo Malaysia on 14 August 2017, "The Creation of Art for Independence Day".

5-14: Kosmo Malaysia on 14 August 2017, "Wan Jamila's Empire of Art".

5-15: Malay Mail Malaysia on 14 August 2017, "Merdeka Theme Brings out Best in Artists".

5-16: Malay Mail Malaysia on 20 September 2017, "Speaking through Art".

I have coached Jamila in art since she was ten (2012). From the time she turned fourteen (2017), I have homeschooled her. Several local artists provide guidance on the technical aspects of fine art to both of us. Jamila draws intricate patterns and human expressions based on her experiences and observations. She also draws her own interpretation of people.

Her special inborn power of imagination and assimilation of patterns and colours makes her art different and unique. She has created a unique genre in the art industry. Most of her drawings are a collection of her memories in terms of her emotions, her passions, and events she has experienced. She creates a unique masterpiece of her memories in the form of collaged patterns. Her paintings are therapeutic. She can move the viewer's emotion, making them smile and feel happy and excited.

She started drawing using pigment ink on acid-free paper and developed into acrylic on canvas and mixed media. Her series of masterpieces are *Three Ladies, Kebaya Girls, Rapunzel, Anora, Fish Mosaic, Teapots, Mermaids, Unity in Diversity* (*Merdeka* and *People of Malaysia*), *Cats, Butterfly*, and many others. Her most popular series is *Fish Mosaic*.

5-17: *Fish Mosaic Series 10: The Art of Togetherness*, 2017

Throughout her artistic journey, she participated in 18 art exhibitions and shares her passion and gifted talent through 23 participation in societies, associations, and various media coverage. Within a year, Artjamila has sold fifty-five original paintings.

Some of her other achievements are:
1. She won a weekly live poster drawing competition at the National Art Gallery, Kuala Lumpur, Malaysia, "Negaraku", 29 July 2017.
2. She has sold fifty-five original paintings from May 2017 to May 2018.
3. Twelve of the original paintings sold were sold to a corporate customer for its corporate calendar 2018.
4. Three of her original paintings were sold to a five-star international hotel.
5. She painted a nine-foot-by-six-foot mural at the second lobby entrance of SMK Seksyen 9, Shah Alam, Selangor.
6. She painted a portrait of the crown prince of Selangor and presented it as a gift to the crown prince on 21 April 2017
7. She was the youngest artist to be featured in the Merdeka Live Art Painting Exhibition at 1Utama Shopping Centre in September 2017.
8. She was appointed as Hulo Artist from 2 February 2018 until 2 February 2019 for Hulo Hotel & Art Gallery (a boutique hotel in Kuala Lumpur that display the works of Malaysia's very best creative talents in its guest rooms and public areas).
9. She registered her business as "Artjamila Gallery" on 28 May 2018 and became a taxpaying citizen at the age of fifteen.

Chapter 6
OPINIONS OF ARTJAMILA'S COLLECTORS

6-1: *Three Ladies Series 2B*, 2017

6-2:
Dato Salleh Yeop
Art Collector
Kuala Lumpur, Malaysia

I was most fascinated by the selection and combination of bright colours as well as her gorgeous interpretation of the hair of her objects by applying smooth and long strokes on varying facial expressions. Jamila is obviously a highly talented girl and I think, given the proper guidance and motivation, she will excel further in the future.

—Dato' Salleh Yeop

6-3: *Three Ladies in Kimono Series 9B*, 2107

6-4:
Mizuan Abdul Manaf
Executive Director
WSBJ Industries Sdn Bhd
Selangor, Malaysia

It was like love at first sight for me with Jamila's art pieces. I was so impressed that I purchased one of her originals the same day. I find her artwork unique and intriguing. While her vibrant choice of contrasting patterns and colours and attention to details are her obvious strengths, it is her simple yet deep portrayal of facial expressions that catches my eyes the most. It didn't take me long to add another one of Jamila's originals to my collection. She is a talented artist with a big future ahead of her.

—Mizuan Abdul Manaf

6-3B: *Rapunzel Series 4B,* 2017

6-5: *Three Ladies in Kebaya Series*

6-6:
TPr. Hj. Ihsan Zainal Mokhtar
President 2017 to 2019
Malaysian Institute of Planners
Malaysia

I find the way Jamila looks at the world beautifully interesting. What she feels is reflected in her paintings through her expression of simple things using vibrant colours and flowing lines. Her drawings are a definite centre of attention for any space that needs one. I'm a proud owner of one of her drawings.

—TPr. Hj. Ihsan Zainal Mokhtar

6-7: *Three Ladies Series 7B*, 2017

6-8:
Ar. Datuk Tan Pei Ing
Principal, PI Architect
Former president of the Malaysian Institute of Architects (PAM)
Former president of the Architects Regional Council Asia (ARCASIA)

I fell in love with the painting as soon as I walked into the gallery. I felt the strong bond with the lovely artist who has expressed tremendous passion through the painting. The display of an array of colours is so well coordinated with great vibrancy and it attracted me instantly. I love the intricate details shown on the hair and clothes and also the jovial smiles of the three young girls, who are really captivating.

—Ar. Datuk Tan Pei Ing

6-10:
Dato' Dr Zalizan Mohd Jelas
Retired Professor of special needs education,
Former dean, faculty of education,
Universiti Kebangsaan Malaysia
Selangor, Malaysia

6-9: *Three Ladies in Kebaya Series 11B*, 2017

When I first saw Jamila's collection of paintings, I was struck by the vibrant colours and attention to details. I am also attracted to a particular theme in her paintings—the three ladies with long wavy hair—which resonates with me as a mother of three daughters. As I know more about Jamila herself and her challenges to communicate and express her ideas and feelings, I am in awe at the gift that was bestowed upon her by the Almighty and the support of her family to realise that precious gift. The *Three Ladies* theme reflects Jamila's happy and strong socio-emotional bond with family members especially with her mother and sister. The family support is vital in the development of communication ability as well as social and emotional growth for people who face those challenges like Jamila.

—Dato' Dr Zalizan Mohd Jelas

6-11: *Rapunzel Series 2B*, 2017

6-12: *Teapots Series 2*, 2017

6-13: *Teapots Series 1*, 2017

6-14: *Three Ladies Series 5B*, 2017

6-15: *Fish Mosaic Series 1*, 2016

6-16: *Malay Traditional Dance: Ulek Mayang, Malaysia Series 1*, 2017

6-17: *Chinese Traditional Dance: Fan Dance, Malaysia Series 1*, 2016

6-18: *Three Ladies in Kimono Series 10B*, 2017

6-19: *Malay Traditional Dance: Zapin, Malaysia Series 1*, 2016

6-20: *Group Photo During Travels Series 2*, 2017

6-21: *Malay Traditional Dance: Gamelan, Malaysia Series 1*, 2016

6-22: *Three Ladies Series 3B*, 2017

6-23: *Corporate Painting MBSB*, 2017

6-24:
Azlina Mohd Rashad
Chief corporate officer
MBSB Bank Berhad
Kuala Lumpur, Malaysia.

I was immediately attracted to the work of Jamila because of the vibrant colours that she had used for her artwork. I became more intrigued when told that the three ladies she draws represent herself, her mother, and her younger sister. That to me was endearing as much as it was heart-warming. As MBSB produces its own calendar every year, I have always wanted something different and Artjamila was definitely the answer. Our table calendar for 2018 represents her thirteen pieces of artwork, and for that, we have been praised with compliments and admiring comments. I am definitely pleased that Jamila's art has fascinated thousands more people, and I wish this amazing girl an abundance of success. I know that the calendar shall become a collector's item one day.

—Azlina Mohd Rashad

6-25: *Mermaid Series 3: Life Beyond Boundaries*, 2018

6-26: *Fish Mosaic Series 14: The Art of Togetherness*, 2018

6-27: *Fish Mosaic Series 15: The Art of Togetherness*, 2018

6-28: *Fish Mosaic Series 16: The Art of Togetherness*, 2018

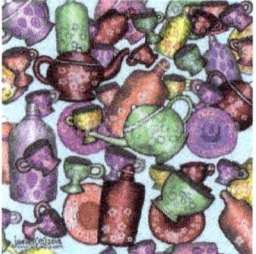
6-29: *Teapots Series 6: The Pleasant Taste of Tea*, 2018

6-30: *Teapots Series 7: The Pleasant Taste of Tea*, 2018

6-31: *Teapots Series 8: The Pleasant Taste of Tea*, 2018

6-32: *Butterflies Series 2: Flying High*, 2018

6-33: *Cats in Pyjamas Series 1*, 2018

6-34: *Cats in Pyjamas Series 2*, 2018

6-35: *The Dance Series 1*, 2018

6-36: *Orchid Series 1*, 2018

6-37: *Cats in Baskets Series 2: The Art of Togetherness*, 2018

6-38: *Cats in Baskets Series 1: The Art of Togetherness*, 2018

6-39:
Rosli Mohd Rose
Chief internal auditor,
Group internal audit department,
Tenaga Nasional Berhad,
Kuala Lumpur, Malaysia

What caught my eyes when I first saw her paintings were the vibrant colours. The choice and combination of the colours were simply perfect. One cannot help but also admire her attention to details. I particularly like the smiles radiating from the faces of the girls and cats in the paintings. They seem to be so contagious that it makes me smile at them too. I find her paintings cheerful and lively. She clearly has a distinctive style, which is unique.
—Rosli Mohd Rose

6-43: *Fish Mosaic Series 13: The Art of Togetherness*, 2018

6-44:
Zaiton Jamaluddin
Art collector
Kuala Lumpur, Malaysia

Jamila's paintings are so neat and colourful as if guided by some inner discipline. Yet they are complex in design with lots of different patterns in them. I am truly enchanted by them. And what is more compelling is the fact that her inability to communicate verbally is more than compensated through her hands with such a work of beauty. Surely, they come from the purest of heart and mind. I am sure I will enjoy her paintings and be mesmerised by the mystery it evokes. It is perhaps a chance to understand her and her work better. I am sure Jamila will go far in the world of art. I do hope to be able to follow her progress in the coming years.

—Zaiton Jamaluddin

6-45: *Fish Mosaic Series 12*, 2017

6-46:
Alice Chang Oi Lai
Art collector and established artist
Kuala Lumpur, Malaysia

The colour combinations of Art Jamila's paintings caught my attention. From her paintings you can feel she is happy and peaceful. She knows how to depict her world through art. She wants to paint her ideal world.

—Alice Chang Oi Lai

6-47: *Rapunzel Series 3B*, 2017

6-48:
Charlie Yap
Founder and chief operating officer
The Hulo Hotel & Gallery
Kuala Lumpur Malaysia

As a hotelier who advocates local artists, it is indeed my pleasure to own, in my opinion, one of the finest pieces that I think defines Jamila as an artist. The lush and colourful vibrant hair, the composition, the aesthetic beauty of the character; transcends the age and passion of a young artist. Congratulations, dear Jamila, and I look forward to your solo show at the Hulo Hotel + Gallery.

—Charlie Yap

6-50:
Ar. Hazlinda Hashim
Principal
RAM architect
Shah Alam, Selangor, Malaysia

Her paintings are well thought in colours combination and simply eye catching to all. She has a unique style and I am looking forward to see her creative journey in her artworks in years to come.

—Ar. Hazlinda Hashim

6-49: *Baskets Series 12: Weaving Our Dreams*, 2018

6-51: *Fish Mosaic Series 11*, 2017

I am very impressed with her talent in using her imagination to produce works of art which are vibrant and colourful. For someone so young, she has potential and I wish her a long and successful career as an artist.

—Tan Sri Dato' Azman Hashim

6-52:
Tan Sri Dato' Azman Hashim
Group chairman
AmBank Group
Kuala Lumpur, Malaysia

Chapter 7

OPINIONS OF ART CURATORS

7-1: Zuriyadi Sarpin Curator National Art Gallery, Malaysia.

A disability need not be viewed as permanent and can be turned into strength. Jamila was diagnosed as autistic at the age of four but now is a well-known artist in the country. Her drawings are being bought by art collectors for personal collection or used to adorn corporate offices. Her drawings stir up emotions of art lovers. Autism is a disability, but with support and nurturing by family members, she has found her niche and is now producing sought-after drawings.

Seeing her work reminds me of Stephen Wiltshire, who also suffers from autism. His photographic mind enables him to draw cityscapes in such great detail that transcends normal minds. He is well known and exhibits his work all over the world. This is God's gift to him.

As with Jamila, her unconventional mind enables her to produce fantastic drawings. Her drawing is based on her emotion, desires and her life experiences. She captures a vision and transforms it into a painting. She has difficulty in verbal communication and uses visual cues as means of communication. This is God's gift to her. At such a young age, she is already producing drawings with complex and complicated elements that reflect her creative and unconventional thinking.

It is my ardent hope that she will become a role model to other children suffering from autism. She could also be a beacon of hope for parents raising autistic children. Turn the disability into strength. I hope that Jamila will continue to grow as an artist and will be famous at the world stage and her paintings will become our national treasures.

—Zuriyadi Sarpin
(Translated by Jemima Shaiful)

7-2:
Wan Muhammad Danial Wan Omar
Project manager
Museum, Art Gallery and Knowledge Management Centre
Central Bank of Malaysia (Bank Negara Malaysia)
Kuala Lumpur, Malaysia

Artjamila's artworks are awesome. They look so beautiful to me. When I first saw her artworks, it completely caught my attention, and I decided to learn more about her work. The colour combination is perfect, and I find the character to be adorable. Jamila possesses a huge talent in the arts, and I believe one day, she will stand with the prominent artists of Malaysia, as well as in the world of art.

—Wan Muhammad Danial Wan Omar

7-3:
Nor Azmi Sulong
Project director and curator of ArtEDecor,
Antara Event Management Sdn Bhd

One look at Artjamila's work tells the viewer that she is no ordinary child. At just fourteen, Jamila is a powerhouse of talent. The start of her art journey manifested as a young child, when she found that, due to her autism, drawing her emotions was easier than physically expressing them. When her talent was inevitably recognised, she began honing her skills with the help of professional artists. Her work is usually themed around multitudes (multitudes of women, fish, etc.), all connected by detailed patterns. Jamila takes great care in depicting every strand of a woman's hair or the scales of a fish. A great sense of beauty can be felt from her paintings. Together with a sensitive use of vibrant yet harmonising colours, Jamila's work is truly mesmerising.

—Nor Azmi Sulong

7-4:
Lum Peng Cheong
Founder, chief executive officer, and curator,
The Art People Gallery

As an avid art collector and curator of a gallery, I am in constant search for young talented artist across Asia. I was very fortunate and delighted to be able to visit Jamila's studio. Her work is truly admirable for such a young talent. Jamila depicts her expressions in her paintings, translating her surroundings into a series of abstract shapes and forms. I believe with such notable talent as a young artist, her work is to look out for! Keep it up Jamila!

Art is not what you see, but what you make others see.

—Edgar Degas
—Lum Peng Cheong

Chapter 8

OPINIONS OF ESTABLISHED ARTISTS

8-1:
Khalid Mohd Sapari
Established artist
Kuala Lumpur, Malaysia

In 2016, I visited Jamila's art studio. Her art equipment seemed to be so carefully organised by her mother. I was inspired when her mother presented to me a compilation of Jamila's work from her early years. I saw great potential in Jamila's early drawings; she truly was born an artist. Her imaginations are wild, and that makes her different and unique. With an assimilation of technical aspects, it gives birth to wonderful art.

—Khalid Mohd Sapari
(translated by Jemima Shaiful)

8-2:
Nur Azmi Mokhtar
a.k.a Mie Mambo
Established artist, writer, and musician
Base: Kuala Lumpur, Malaysia

While at the Faculty of Art and Design at UiTM, I was told by lecturers that "art is an institution". That's how I look at Jamila's special masterpieces. Initially when I looked at her works of art, I did not think they were produced by a teenager with autism. I can honestly say that Jamila is capable of producing quality artwork, like the work of a professional artist. Jamila's works consist of varying lines, and she uses bright colours and feminine subjects. I guess the imagery of beautiful women in her work is her and her mother, who continuously gives full support to and concentration on Jamila. Some of Jamila's works illustrate the subjects we have at home, such as teapots and baskets. This is called "visual documentation", which greatly helps her to master her drawings.

I have known her since early 2017, and I've noticed the progress in her artistic work. I love her art because her paintings can be a subject of discussion of "naive art" or "outsider art". The ideas in her art can go beyond the limited sight of a specific terminology. She falls under the category of fine art artist and relates to the meaning of "art is an institution". We can analyse the subject matter of her art in terms of the texture, forms, and shapes she uses. We are curious as to how Jamila gave birth to the magical artwork from her interpretation of the subjects in her mind. I am confident that Jamila will continue to add her magic to her work.

—Mie Mambo
(translated by Jemima Shaiful)

8-3:
Jamal Tommy
Established watercolour artist
Kuala Lumpur, Malaysia

I was very amazed at Jamila's abilities. She is as amazing as the amount of talent she possesses. I have been following her on Facebook and reading through articles published on Artjamila in the newspaper. After getting the opportunity to see Artjamila's works at the 2018 ArtEDecor event, my heart continued to whisper, "This child can go far, both in Malaysia and internationally." I am amazed at how this special child can create such interesting compositions in each of her works. Every piece of art on display can tether the observer's heart. I am sure that every piece of Artjamila's work is and was born of a sincere and honest heart. Artjamila's art stays close to my heart.

8-4:
Wan Borhanuddin Md Noor
Established Malaysian watercolour artist specialising in landscapes
Base: Kuala Lumpur, Malaysia

There is such a maturity in Artjamila's artwork, which can be seen in her use of both warm and cool colours that are balanced brilliantly throughout her works. Her compositions may appear busy at first, but through the use of repetitive motifs coloured in different tones and hues, they provide enough depth and space to please the observer. Her creativity and boldness can also be seen in the hairs of female figures she drew in all colours except black. Artjamila has so much to say through her masterpieces that reflects how she views the world, that of a joyful, cheerful, and thankful person.

—Wan Borhanuddin Md Noor

8-5:
Zaharin Mohammad
Established abstract expressionist
Kuala Lumpur, Malaysia

Looking at Jamila's works is like looking at something that has been produced by a fine art university graduate. It is absolutely unexpected that she is actually a fifteen-year-old autistic child. Jamila's work is of the naive art genre. Her talent and persistence produce work like a professional. The way she plays with the design elements such as colour, line, shape, texture, and space are so dramatic, and it fulfils the principles of design that create balance, contrast, pattern, and variety. She expresses her feelings on the canvas through the use of repetitive images of her surroundings. Jamila produces astonishing works of art without formal art training. May this heavenly child continue to be bloom in her art and be successful internationally, God willing.

—Zaharin Mohammad
(translated by Jemima Shaiful)

8-6:
Abey Zoul
Established watercolour artist and author
Abey Zoul's Watercolour Techniques
Base: Kuala Lumpur, Malaysia

Art Jamila's works leave me with an impression of wonder. It is clear from the way she draws that she has talent. It has been a year since I have discovered this child's works, and as she is known to be different from others of her age. I am in awe of what she can do. The emotions spoken in her art are clear, and they have the ability to move my soul. I frequently ask myself how a special child like her could possibly produce something this perfect from the mere strokes of her drawing tools. The compositions, the colours, the stories behind every one of her paintings, and all the other elements in her art complement each other so well, giving proof of how she has mastered the art of drawing. Congratulations and well done to Jamila and her mother, Noorhashimah. Continue working with your artistic flair and shake the world.

—Abey Zoul
(translated by Jemima Shaiful)

8-7:
Rizalman Misran (Ryzal Mysran)
Established watercolour artist and
graphic designer
Base: Kuala Lumpur, Malaysia

All human beings are born with a special gift endowed by God, with a "sixth sense", in other words, "autism" characters. If these extraordinary abilities can be detected at a very young age, as well as polished properly and perfectly, they would be able to donate something special to the community and country. Jamila, to me, is the most beautiful gift. Her memory is so delicate and sharp, and when it is translated wholeheartedly onto the canvas or a piece of paper, she produces it so sincerely and thoroughly into a masterpiece. Her works are admired by art lovers and are a fascination of people who appreciate special children like her. Congratulations to the parents and family for their great effort in bringing her up to this level. I am very confident that there will be more successes in her life. Hopefully, Jamila will continue to succeed and become an icon in the world of art nationally and internationally, Congratulations!

—Ryzal Mysran

8-8:
Nor Hanem Mohd Nor
Established artist
Owner, Nem Studio
Kuala Lumpur, Malaysia

Different from other artists, Jamila has gained a style in her paintings even at a very young age. Her technique and style of drawing are in line with the idea and message she wants to deliver. She spontaneously paints as though there had been a shadow in her mind. The combined warmth of femininity and her everyday life is illustrated with warmth and harmony in her paintings. The Almighty's grace for Jamila is unique.

—Nor Hanem Mohd Nor
(translated by Jemima Shaiful)

8-9:
Abdullah Harun
Established realistic artist
Base: Shah Alam, Selangor

Art Jamila is one of the newly flourishing talents that exist in the crowd of millions of artistic activists in the country (Malaysia). It wouldn't be an exaggeration to say that Artjamila's birth was a godsend to the lovers of art, both locally and from around the world. The reason I say that is because she didn't have any form of art education to enable her talent be noticed. She was only fourteen years of age when she started to take her work professionally. And what's interesting is the way she draws, which is different in a good way from the rest. I believe that, with continuous exposure and opportunity, she will continue to advance and improve in the technique of painting. I wish Wan Jamila success. Hopefully, with her talent and support from her family, especially her mother, she will be able to go further on both local and international levels.

—Abdullah Harun
(translated by Jemima Shaiful)

8-10:
Abu Zaki Hadri
Established abstract artist
President, Perupa, 2017–2018
Base: Kuala Lumpur, Malaysia

When I was told to give a bit of words on Jamila by her mother, I was struck speechless. All the power God has given her is great, so what else is there to say? Jamila, however a child she may be, is excellent in her own way. The first time I met Jamila and her mother, I was amazed. This girl is very special, and her mother is a wise and visionary woman who has become the backbone of her daughter's success. Her mother has found her talents, and without delay, she has managed to uncover those talents. Every work produced by her has its own storyline and emotion. From my ignorant eyes, I can see that Jamila tells a lot about her experiences and surroundings through her art. The plain colours she uses come straight from her pure heart. She lets her fingers dance purposely over her canvas, with the company of her sharp mind. I was and am amazed at how Jamila can work in her own way. It would be no wonder if her works were able to cheer and delight anyone who sees them. To Jamila's mother, please continue your efforts to guide and to bring your special girl towards success. Do not look back. Congratulations! May your journey become an inspiration to others. I am so proud of you and will continue to be Jamila's fan forever.

—Abu Zaki Hadri
(translated by Jemima Shaiful)

Noorhashimah Mohamed Noordin

8-11:
Mazlan Noor Along
Established abstract artist and poet
Cottage Gemahati, Kajang, Malaysia

We are all gifted in many ways, as that has been God's intention for us from the start. Though we may have been blinded to these gifts and considered them a nuisance at one point, useless and unworthy, we were yet to know of the good it would bring us. Humans are like the glittering stars in the sky; some are brilliance awaiting admiration, and some are too dim to see, a star before its bloom. Every waking minute, every dawning second, we, the stars, tend to forget our purpose, as our gifts remain blind to us.

One star among us has shone her brightest. Artjamila has managed to unleash her full potential, using the gifts she was given. She has given her all to the public, and put herself on a level with other artists of the same brightness as her all around the globe. Even with the weight of her disabilities on her shoulders, she has never let them stop her from achieving her goals. With the guidance and help that her mother gives her, she was able to find her way out of darkness to the light that shines brighter with every ounce of confidence she attains through her path to success. This has given her the courage to be as special as the most ordinary children of her age out there. As time passes, her abilities in art flourish, as she continues to hold onto her ever-growing potential. This is the guidance a mother can give to her beloved child—guidance to a path of sublime beauty and happiness. As humans, we live lives filled with countless tests that will eventually lead us to our own fates one day, depending on the choices we make along the way. Those who understand that every happening has a reason embedded in it from the very beginning will be able to face the negative upbringings fate attempts to throw at us. Although life might not be deemed perfect then, the definition of perfect itself will change in time as we each start to accept our life as it is and make the best out of it. To the dearest Artjamila, please remember that God is always near us and pray that you will always succeed in your work, and hope that you never bat an eye to the precious gift that God has given you. God is very happy when we make use of the gifts that He has given to us. The choice is in our hands whether we decide to be jewels or glass.

—Mazlan Noor Along
(translated by Jemima Shaiful)

Chapter 9
OPINIONS OF ART LOVERS

9-1: *The Malaysian Flag* Series 1, 2017

9-2:
Maheswari Thanapalasingam
Deputy director
Museum, Art Gallery and Knowledge Management Centre,
Central Bank of Malaysia (Bank Negara Malaysia)
Kuala Lumpur, Malaysia.

I saw a glimpse of the "Malaysian Flag" artwork, and I was intrigued to know more about the artist who had so painstakingly created this marvellously intricate piece of work. The minute dots, strokes of paint, and splashes of colour had all come together in unison to create a beautiful work of art depicting the wonderful and indomitable spirit of Merdeka. There stood three beautiful girls, each resplendent in a kebaya, cheongsam, and sari with their long tresses in vivid hues of red flowing into infinity from a vibrant blue and yellow bun conjuring an artful image of our majestic Malaysian flag. Standing in her little booth at the Bank Negara Malaysia 2017 Art Bazaar was a shy and hesitant Jamila. As she greeted me, her soft delicate hands gently clasping mine, this immensely talented child, surely God's gift to the art industry, captured an everlasting place in my heart.

—Maheswari Thanapalasingam

9-3:
Dr Ralph Richard Klemp
President and chief executive officer
Dunia Consulting Group
International business consulting
International mergers and acquisitions

How can you not become a fan of Jamila's iconic paintings? They are so joyful and playful yet so incredibly precise. Jamila has learned to use her special talents with a remarkable sensibility. Her subjects, be it the fairy tales of Rapunzel or the dancing lessons at school, are truly inspiring, giving the viewer a break from oppressive adulthood. However, maybe the most amazing part of Jamila is her mother, Noorhashimah, who has dedicated her life to organising Jamila to become a star. It is Noorhashimah's relentless work and absolute dedication that propels Jamila to more and more stunning artworks. The success of Jamila's paintings is a well-deserved tribute to hard work and unfaltering dedication.

—Dr Ralph R. Klemp

9-4:
Ar. Lillian Tay
Principal and director
Veritas Design Group
Vice president of the Malaysian
Institute of Architects (PAM)

9-5: *Fish Mosaic Series 4*, 2016

A Quiet Fearlessness

For a young artist, Jamila stands out for having so early in her artistic journey developed a distinctive personal style. While her work is often her own personal extension of familiar children's stories, the unhesitant fluidity of her lines and sureness of hand reveal a quiet confidence and fearlessness beyond her years. Her artistic vision shows an intriguing combination of opposing impulses—simple colours, repetitive lines and shapes are patiently and meticulously woven into a myriad of lines and patterns, creating a complex whole. There is a sense of movement and weightlessness in the forms and narratives she creates, which floats yet effortlessly fills the frame of her canvas.

Perhaps her artistic vision is a reflection of the world she resides in, immersed in the half-fantasy realm of the child yet steadily anchored and attuned with the practical demands of everyday life. Her discipline, consistency, and perseverance would be hard to match among her peers in young adulthood. Surely and quietly, Jamila looks set to move to greater heights.

—Ar. Lillian Tay

9-6:
Jumie Al Idid
Founder
Artists in Schools Malaysia

The term "disabled" is subjective. Isn't everyone disabled in one way or another? Different, perhaps. Disabled, I am unsure. Einstein reportedly couldn't even tie his own shoes. Perhaps instead of giving her sympathy, I should sympathise myself. Looking at Jamila's artworks, one can be forgiven for believing that the artist is a so-called normal human being, like the most of us. Her works are definitely—but unsurprisingly—an out-of-the-box gem. She brings me to a completely different dimension, another feeling within my heart that brings new meanings to this world of mine.

I love it when a person is absorbed in doing what he or she loves doing. Jamila seems to be enjoying herself to the fullest, indifferent to what's happening around her. The joy she experiences is what matters, especially for a teen. One can see her painting her inner life, arranging the colours crystallised by pure passion and wild imaginings. Her work is very self-expressive and diverse. One watching her draw could feel that she paints not to satisfy anybody but purely out of heart, which is quite unique for someone of her age. The colours and shapes of her paintings are marvellously adjusted and aligned. They are like the still lives of small cities blown up in scale so beautiful you want to enter them. Anything from the heart would travel to other hearts. Even if it is something emotionally harsh, it's sincere, from the heart. Unless you don't have one, you could probably still feel the love and honesty, whether it is a dead silence or a crazy scream. So, am I, the most imperfect creature, the disabled one?"

—Jumie Al Idid

9-7:
May Ki Wong
Director
Group hospitality
Iktisas Hotels and Resorts
Selangor, Malaysia

When I stumbled across her (Jamila's drawings), I was awestruck with the complexity of patterns, lines, and colours which composed into artworks that exude such a level of innocence, serenity, and love. The attempt to grasp the message from her artwork is most interesting, as most of her drawings are young girls in traditional apparel. The biggest inspiration from her artwork is her self-confidence and appreciation of her roots, which I believe translated from her parents' relentless love and the willpower to educate her. From my perspective, it is beyond an autistic child's artwork; it is the heart and soul of her family.

—May Ki Wong

9-8:
Ruby Ann Phillip
Psychologist
Manipal Hospital Klang
Selangor, Malaysia

I was privileged to be acquainted with Jamila through an event that I had arranged at Manipal Hospitals Klang. Initially introduced by a mutual friend, Noorhashimah (Jamila's mum was quick to accept my invitation to share her extraordinary mother-child relationship with Jamila). Besides sharing insights of honing the skills of an autistic child, Noorhashimah was determined to advocate awareness on the autism spectrum disorder to the public at large. My encounter with Jamila has been nothing short of amazing. Each meeting was memorable and special, leaving me often gaping in awe at her creativity and artistic skills. Her distinctive style shines through every piece of her artwork. Jamila as a person is beautiful, gifted, talented, and a blessing by Almighty. My best wishes to her in all her future endeavours.

—Ruby Ann Phillip

Noorhashimah Mohamed Noordin

9-9:
Hishamuddin Mohamed
Director business development
Lipidware Sdn Bhd
Selangor, Malaysia

The first time I encountered Jamila's work was at the 1 Utama Shopping Complex. It was a typical working day, and I was heading to the parking lot when I saw a poster on the wall with her work. This is no exaggeration, but I was pleasantly stopped in my tracks by the sheer purity of her lines. Effortlessly confident. Each line a part of a story Jamila had to tell … and that is the best part of Jamila's art … They are magic, and they are her stories, and we are lucky to witness her stories. I look forward to her growth and maturity. Let the art world know … Jamila is here.

—Hishamuddin Mohamed

Chapter 10

PEOPLE WHO WERE WITH ME THROUGH MY HARDEST TIMES ON THIS JOURNEY

This journey can be very lonely without the presence of friends to give words of comfort, encouragement and positive energy to keep me going through my darkest hour. I feel blessed to have friends who have come to rescue me at a time when I needed them most. They are like my strong pillars of support who make me believe in my inner strength and that, even during bleak moments, there is light at the end of the tunnel, and every cloud has a silver lining, God willing. I have never looked back since then. I owe them the world and sincerely would like to rejoice in this happy moment with them.

10-1:
Yasmin Kassim
A friend for more than thirty-eight years

Shima. As a friend, she is fiercely loyal to the few who she trusts. As a classmate, she is hardworking, creative, studious, talented, funny, competitive—the one who gets the "gold medal". As a professional, she is a business-minded strategist, maybe shrewd but respected and admired by many. As a wife/parent, she is loving, firm, and responsible, and like a tiger mum, she only wants the best for her kids. One would have to be blessed with her qualities to take on and conquer life's challenges well like she has done and continues to do. She is a fighter, in many ways.

—Yasmin Kassim

10-2:
Ar. Associate Professor (Retired)
Ong Suan Huah
Lecturer and colleague

I was given the opportunity to teach Shima from 1979 till 1983 in MARA Institute of Technology, ITM (now UiTM). She was a model architectural student and showed great potential to be a successful architect. In her graduating year, she received the top student award for the Diploma in Architecture programme.

In 1990 after completing her master's degree in architecture, Shima joined UiTM as a lecturer in the architectural department. As a lecturer, she actively and continuously strived for excellence in her teaching career and received a "Best Performance Award" in 1995. Another feather to her cap was her public lectures on her "pet" topic—fire safety and prevention in buildings.

Single-handedly, Shima nurtured her elder son with lots of love and care. He is now a qualified medical doctor specialising in family medicine. Now, she is given a very blessed and golden opportunity to focus her boundless energy on her special needs daughter, Jamila. I have faith in her to actively strive for an astounding success in all her future goals.

—Ar. Associate Professor (Retired) Ong Suan Huah

10-3:
Sum Mooi Soo
Renew Earth-Life Therapy Centre

Shima is a career-minded person and always gives her best at anything she does. Since 2009, she would usually come to me for a therapeutic massage due to strains caused by stress. This was the result of balancing a demanding double profession and help for her autistic daughter on her shoulders. She looked to me like she always had health problems. Shima would share with me stories of her daily educational activities that she has with her children with me during our massage sessions. I found her life to be somewhat outstanding and something to be proud of. There were times when I would have a vision of her doing something different in her career, neither as an architect nor an associate professor.

As a friend, I would always remind her that Jamila was a special gift sent by the Almighty to her. And that gift came with a responsibility. Shima is the chosen one to perform this task of raising this child and to understand her daughter, because Jamila will be the one to guide her and teach her instead. Jamila will teach Shima the practice of tolerance, patience, perseverance, and the giving of unconditional love. Shima has finally made her choice to change her career path after all these years to concentrate on her daughter more and share her success with the community of autism and the society at large.

—Sum Mooi Soo

10-4:
Associate professor (Sr)
Hasmawati Harun CQS
My colleague at the university

Artjamila: The History in the Making

In our lives, we cross our paths for a reason. The day Ar. Associate Professor (Retired) Noorhashimah met me at my house, she was at the crossroad of her life between balancing her careers with her role as a devoted mom. She came to me after witnessing my journey raising my child against all odds, my son without any formal primary education, making a breakthrough in his academics and social well-being. I have my own story sealed deep in my heart, but to say the least, my son was an underprivileged kid. And later during his teenage life, he earned numerous awards of excellence at schools and at the national level. He even made the headline cover story of the newspaper—totally unexpected but worth every single minute of sacrifices, commitment, and devotion as a mom and hard work on the part of my son. Patience, perseverance, and persistent and plenty of prayers were my anchors in raising my child. In our lives, sometimes we need to sacrifice … like a burning candle to light up a dark room, and we also need to set our priorities. At the beginning of our journey, we might not yet see the light at the other sides of the tunnel; slowly, later we could gain the fruits of our labour of love. That is exactly what happened in my case. I sincerely hope that holds true in her case too.

After a long conversation at my house, I remember telling Ar. Associate Professor (Retired) Noorhashimah, "You will not regret giving your all to your child. Believe me, the journey is bitter, as progress is slow, but the outcome is so sweet that it will make you cry with tears of joy. … You have to go into the playing field and coach her yourself and never give up! The 'good things' don't happen overnight; it needs to be nurtured with kinder love and care.

Honestly, I never doubt a second that Ar. Associate Professor (Retired) Noorhashimah could do greatness, knowing how strong-willed a lady she is, coupled with her gifted skills and abilities. To me, she could nurture a cocoon to become a butterfly in the most epic way.

The rest is history. Looking at the talented young lady of hers, Jamila, she has come a long way and created history of her own, more than any other kids of her age (even adults for that matter). Jamila is a household name to be remembered for a long time. Her artwork is not like any artwork that is just ordinary; it has story, it has soul, and it captures angles beyond imagination. For me, it is magical! Having her own mom as manager come advisor, teacher (you name it), she has flown high and spread her wings. To the proud mother, kudos to you, my dear sister, and this is what I have left to say: "Now it's your turn to spread the words of love and wisdom that may change other people's lives." Heartiest congratulation to Artjamila and the family. Bravo for the publication of this book. Lets rejoice this moment by thanking God the Almighty for the wonderful blessing in our lives.

—Associate Professor Sr. Hasmawati Harun CQS

Noorhashimah Mohamed Noordin

10-5:
Munirah Abd Mutalib
An architect friend since 2013

To write about Artjamila, I have to begin with my journey of how I first met Jamila's famous mom, Ar. Associate Professor (Retired) Noorhashimah Mohamed Noordin (Shima). We first met as fellow lecturers when I was assigned to be in Shima's studio group design team, where she was the head of the final year First Degree Architectural Design Studio back in Uitm Shah Alam in 2013.

Our friendship blossomed beyond the studio teaching session when Shima and I started to read our Al Quran together during lunch break in her little lecturer's office. We then continued to read after lecture hours in Shima's architectural office practice, where I was first introduced to Jamila and Jemima. After a few Al Quran reading sessions during their after-school hours, I became Jamila and Jemima's Quran teacher.

I was inspired with awe at how well-ordered and professionally organised Shima's private and professional life was and still is. Yet, her natural gift of motherhood instincts surpasses any fellow mothers I've met, may they be among my fellow architects, lecturers, and friends. Her relentless passion above all as a mother, to both Jamila and Jemima, is much desired and inspirational. This, I believe, is the birth of Artjamila.

Artjamila is a journey of unconditional love and celebration of a special family having to embrace the world of autism. It is a result of full conviction and commitment in pursuing deeply into the mind and heart of the secret world of autism. Artjamila is a door leading us into the beginning of a whole new world—a beautiful, colourful, intriguing, mysterious, and unique world.

The world-where the "randomness of life" collides and clashes with an individual's need for the sameness.
—Eilean Miller

It is... a bright thread in the rich tapestry of life.
—Tony Astwood

This inspiring journey of ArtJamila is best summarised through the following wise words:

Hardship and ease walk hand-in-hand in this world. Embracing them both as being from the same benevolent source ensures that we walk with gratitude for our blessings, and gratefulness for our challenges.
—Sheikh Hamza Yusuf
—Munirah Abd Mutalib

10-6:
Dr Imanul Hassan Abdul Shukor
Son of Noorhashimah Noordin

As an elder brother, I was very excited when I knew my mother was pregnant. I was fourteen at that moment, and I was the only child back then, after my two brothers had passed away. The birth of Jamila brought a new source of happiness, and I remember the first time I held her in my arms; it was one of the most unforgettable moments in my life.

I was there all the time to see Jamila grow up till her kindergarten years. The courage, sacrifices, and determinations of my mother, Ar. Associate Professor (Retired) Noorhashimah Noordin, during those challenging times of raising an autistic child were overwhelming. I had never seen a working mother who could juggle between a hectic life of a never-ending workload as an established architect and the numerous classes that were to be conducted as a university associate professor and also the struggle to nurture an autistic daughter at home. She is one of a kind.

Most mothers with autistic offspring either retire early or halt their career progression to focus on their special child. Special praise to those mothers who have made those big decisions for the sake of their child. But my mother is unique. She was able to start an architectural firm and make it successful. Apart from that, she was also a respected lecturer in her faculty. And with all that hard work and those sleepless nights completing her unfinished projects and architectural drawings, she was even able to entertain and raise her special daughter by herself! Wow.

Regarding Artjamila, she recognised the talent of Jamila since she was a small kid. From then, she nurtured Jamila to be successful in painting. She told me once that she saw that Jamila's future was in art. And the rest is history. She successfully brought up Jamila from scratch, guiding Jamila to success, and currently, Artjamila is a renowned artist, mostly due to the great tutelage of our forward-thinking mother.

She inspired me to be the best and to be successful in life, even if there were numerous obstacles ahead. Today I am a medical doctor at a primary health clinic, currently pursuing a family medicine postgraduate course. I am grateful to have a supermom like her.

—Dr Imanul Hassan Abdul Shukor

I was even more blessed to have my youngest daughter, Jemima, helping me to care for Jamila continuously throughout this journey.

10-7:
2 September 2007
Jemima (4)
Jamila (5)

10-8:
8 September 2007
Jemima (4)
Jamila (5)

10-9:
08 September 2007
Jemima (4)
Jamila (5)

10-10:
01 October 2008
Jemima (5)
Jamila (6)

10-11:
29 March 2009
Jemima (6)
Jamila (7)

10-12:
29 March 2009
Jemima (6)
Jamila (7)

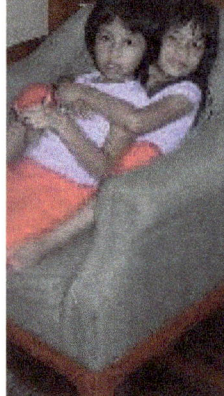

10-13:
23 September 2009
Jemima (6)
Jamila (7)

10-14:
15 March 2010
Jemima (7)
Jamila (8)

10-15:
19 June 2010
Jemima (7)
Jamila (8)

10-16:
10 November 2012
Jemima (9)
Jamila (10)

10-17:
10 November 2012
Jemima (9)
Jamila (10)

10-18:
15 January 2012
Jemima (9)
Jamila (10)

Chapter 11

CONCLUSION: WORDS OF ADVICE AND THE WAY AHEAD

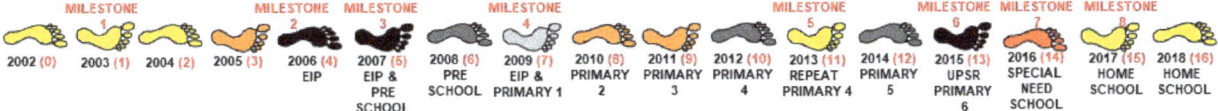

11-1: The footprints of my journey

This documented journey has taught me:
1. To see things from a different perspective
2. To learn to look at things/issues beyond what the naked eye can see
3. To get out from the standard mould of teaching
4. That art is a therapy
5. To treasure memories (The slogan for Jamila's paintings is "Masterpiece of Memories").
6. To see the magical strength of willpower

In conclusion, my step-by-step journey and all the important milestones can be concluded as written in this final chapter.

We need to be observant of the children in our care from the moment of their birth, and we should not take things for granted. It is all right to compare the development between siblings since their birth. In our case, we were lucky to have been gifted with another younger child, Jemima. The younger one's actions were compared to the elder, and so we were able to identify the inabilities of the elder from there.

Life was very challenging due to the weight of my responsibilities—that is, handling my profession with an autistic child in my hands. We need to regard the challenges we are faced with as an opportunity to lead our lives to the path that is right for us and the people we are close to. The reward that will come out of this is sure to be enormous. Friends are one of the most important things that life can give us. Cherish them to the fullest.

Of all possessions, a friend is the most precious.
—Herodotus

Treasure the family that stay by your side through thick and thin. We should always be thankful for their presence from when they weren't absent in our desperate times of need.

The family is one of nature's masterpieces.
—George Santayana

Explore the possibilities of your children's potential. Give them all the support they need. A variety of materials, like art tools, and technology, such as a tablet, should be presented to them (with controls on usage, of course) to let them explore their inborn talents. We need to give our children an amount of space for them to trust us, as we should trust them. Jamila, for example, communicated using the strokes of her fingers as they glided across the screen of her tablet. She used to draw digitally to express herself and to put her emotions on display in an attempt to make everyone understand her more. And we did.

The past, like the future, is indefinite and exists only as a spectrum of possibilities.
—Stephen Hawking

Intervention centres are important assets to the lives of children like Jamila. But keep in mind that not all intervention centres will work with every child. Monitor your child's progress. And show your sensitive side to your child and towards their actions, however ridiculous they may act upon attending the chosen centre. Do not force your child. Rather, be gentle with him or her and be by his or her side. Firstly, I advise that you study the concept of operation of the chosen intervention centre. This should be done before and during the early sessions of intervention. Some centres operate to the best of their own interests and not that of the child, so take note of that. Frequently switching from centre to centre may be inefficient; it is best to do so only when the child has reached the limit of his or her abilities.

In Jamila's case, however, we had to move her from one intervention centre to another multiple times. Each centre had its own strengths. But when we saw Jamila had stopped progressing after she had reached her limit, we had no choice but to pull her from the centres and move on instead. We managed to identify her feelings, and so we decided it best to follow her feelings and desires in making our decisions.

We made the very fortunate decision of sending Jamila to private school during her primary school years. The school provided an inclusive program for children with special needs, and we thought that to be fit for a child like her. After some time in the program, we saw a lot of improvement in her in terms of her academic and social capabilities.

However good that is, though, parents must not solely depend on the school and expect miracles to happen. Parents must play an important role by guiding their special child personally at home, especially when it comes to following through on the activities and homework given by the school. Treasure every moment with your child because time is precious. Family members should always be at the ready to sacrifice their time and accept the situation at hand regarding a child's needs together; they must not complain and call what has been given to them a burden.

Take note of what your children are doing once they are home from school. Do not force them to follow the norm, whereby children must come home with notes on the subjects taught in school. Accept them well, even if they come back with drawings in their schoolbooks. This is an alarm bell to you that your child is different than the other children. Therefore, you need to change from your standard mould of doing things. Your method of doing things has to change. This is because the child is telling you that he or she thinks differently—as Jamila does; she sees things in ways that others might find unimaginable. She isn't linguistic. Rather, she is a visual thinker. She holds information in ways that people will hardly understand. One part of her brain functions more than the other part.

Always explore and research facilities and services available to improve your child. Consider things like craniosacral massage therapy, dyslexia centres for reading, and so on. Jamila had her sense of touch improved after attending sessions of craniosacral massage therapy. Jamila learned how to read with sessions at a dyslexic centre, not an autistic centre. The lesson learned is do not limit your opportunity to centres for autism only. Explore and discover. It will surprise you.

The best teacher is always the parent. Parents must sacrifice and learn what children learn in school. Relate what they learn to daily activities. Math and science can be applicable to daily activities. For example, the subject of division relates to cutting a cake into several pieces. This process of learning is more efficient and applicable to children with different abilities.

At the end of the day, the most overwhelming key to a child's success is the positive involvement of parents.
—Jane D. Hull

Do not ignore any signs of distress from your child. Instead, investigate and think of a remedy. And take immediate action. Help your child. Jamila was not happy when she was in standard 4 because she was bullied by her classmates. I decided to retain her at standard 4 the following year and join the studious class, where the children are more understanding and accept her. I saw progress after that.

Participate with parents who have similar problems as you. Team up and do something for the sake of your child. For example, do revision classes together. Encourage your child to participate in school activities and events like concerts and the like. It is likely that you will notice a development in your child. Your child might surprise you with his or her abilities—if they are tied with the activity he or she participated in, of course.

Correction does much, but encouragement does more.
—Johann Wolfgang von Goethe

Do not underestimate your child. I have underestimated Jamila in the past. I expected she would get an E on science during her UPSR examinations. But surprisingly, she got a C instead. Do not be afraid to take drastic action. Evaluate the situation. Make decisions based on what is best for your child, because he or she has a long way to go in life, as opposed to you. Imagine the regrets you will have if you don't take action now.

Trust me, the reward is enormous. The satisfaction is great. The happiness is wonderful. Remember, your child is your responsibility, a gift, not a burden. Even if you are on top of the world with your profession, make that important move. Remember that we are born into this world with a duty destined by the Almighty. And so take it with an open heart. You will be rewarded. The most difficult decision I made was to retire from all my professional duties; indeed it was the best decision. Now I feel fulfilled.

All parents builds hope when they send their child to a school or a programme. If the programme does not match your child's needs, don't be afraid to change your route and destination. It might be a blessing in disguise, which will lead you to a better opportunity. The test is an alarm bell, waking you up to the fact that you are on the wrong track. So every misfortune can be for a better fortune.

The curriculum of the government's school programme in the special needs centre I sent Jamila to in 2016 was too low for her. The government's inclusive mainstream programme, however, was too high for her. As such, the government school was not a suitable place for Jamila. A homeschool programme instead matched her needs.

In August 2016, I was diagnosed with colon cancer and had to undergo two major operations. This was a wake-up call for me to be more alert about my diet and lifestyle and live a healthier life. This was also a wake-up call for me to look back into my earlier objective for Jamila, which was to help her follow the mainstream and go through the normal system of education like other normal children. Initially, I had wanted Jamila to start from the bottom, to sit for the government examinations, enter university, and have a profession like others.

The long recovery period following the major operation I had to go through caused me to lose time for Jamila's academic activities. I could not rewind the clock. At this point, I decided to make a bigger decision. I would concentrate on her strength—on helping her to do what she could do, rather than what she could not do. I decided to work on her talent as an artist when she was fourteen years old (in 2016).

At this milestone, do not be afraid to divert your route again. Take a better route. Do not be afraid to explore. You will have a lot of surprises ahead of you. In less than a year, Jamila blossomed as an artist. Jamila chose to express her art in the form of unique patterns and styles, creating a fresh genre in the art industry. Her way of drawing shines in every piece of her work, each in its own little way. Her paintings can be declared as a sort of therapy. As one of Jamila's art collectors stated, as he looks at all the smiling faces of the girls in her paintings, he cannot help but smile back. This shows that Jamila has the ability to move the emotions of the people who see her paintings, like flowers swaying in the wind. They feel happy, they feel excited, and they smile. Her art is, overall, a pleasing sight to be seen.

Artjamila's collectors are impressed and are enchanted with her talent and her ability to use her imagination to produce works of art that are vibrant and colourful, with attention to intricate details and flowing lines. Her simple yet deep portrayal of jovial facial expressions catches their eyes. They like the smiles radiating from the faces of the girls and cats in the paintings. Surely, the work of beauty come from the purest of heart and mind. They enjoy her painting and are mesmerised by the mystery it evokes.

Jamila captures a vision in her memories and transforms it into a magical artwork. She spontaneously paints as though there had been a shadow in her mind, and she shares the pureness of her heart with the viewers to capture her message. With every piece of art that Jamila produces, she is telling us that life is all about making memories. Today's sweet moments become tomorrow's precious memories. The five things we cannot recover in life are:

> a stone after it is thrown,
> a word after it is said,
> an occasion after it is missed,
> time after it is gone, and
> trust after it is lost.

Therefore, treasure all the important moments, because memories are golden. These are some examples of Jamila's paintings that reflect her memories.

My Journey with Artjamila

11-2:
Three Ladies Series 13B: Memories Are Golden, 2018
To Jamila, the *Three Ladies* was inspired by the memories of all the precious moments spent with her mother and younger sister.

11-4:
Anora Series 1B, 2016
This portrait resembles Jamila's character as graceful. Many art lovers have said that this painting moves their emotion.

11-3:
Cats in Baskets Series 2: The Art of Togetherness, 2018
Watching cats playing with woven baskets is fun and inspires happiness. Jamila enjoyed painting series of cats in baskets whenever she missed her cats dearly.

11-5:
Cats in Pyjamas Series 1, 2018
Jamila loves to draw cats to remind her of her adorable beloved cats.

I am glad Jamila has progressed well since the year she was diagnosed with ADHD and showing symptoms of autism. From being non-verbal, she became verbal. From being completely restless and hyperactive, she became calm and graceful. From being unable to give attention to a task presented, she became able to focus on the tasks given to her more than most people can, especially when she paints. From not being able to perform self-help skills, she can now perform household duties and is even diligent in performing her daily tasks. Once very dependent on others, she can now be independent when it comes to many aspects of tasks and duties. Once in her own world, she can now socialise with people and respond to questions well. And finally, once constantly nervous, she is now more well composed and can take instructions without much hassle.

11-13:
Jamila at 15 years old.

11-16:
Jamila at 15 years old.

I started my travels with an autistic child in darkness. Fortunately, as the saying goes, we only see light in darkness. Without darkness, the stars can't shine. My journey is not an ordinary one. It is an experimental and exciting discovery. This journey has taught me to see things from a different perspective. It has taught me to learn to look at things beyond what the naked eye can see. There are many ways to perform a task and to arrive at a destination. Since Jamila has a different kind of ability, I decided I should not follow the normal route that ordinary children take. Instead of going "bottom up" in order to help her achieve a profession, I took a "top-down" approach, following the opposite route. I applied a learning system that was centred towards her. I customised the approach to enable Jamila to learn productively.

We should learn to embrace our children as who they are and help them to find their grid in life naturally. It is of utmost importance to show respect for a child who has greatness ahead of him or her and who can continue to grow with dignity and respect for who he or she is. Prioritise your children's needs and talents so that they can have the opportunity to have as natural a life as possible. Autism did not stop Einstein, Mozart, Newton, or Temple Grandin from reaching the stars.

Life is like a book. Some chapters are sad, some are happy, and some are exciting. But if you never turn the page, you will never know what the next chapter has in store for you. My next chapter is to move forward into the second phase of my journey, with more improvements and achievements for my daughter. I especially want to focus on her ability to survive on her own and to be independent. I am exploring the use of artificial intelligence software to improve her cognitive ability and improve the content of her curriculum with a more structured timetable. The discoveries of this adventure will be documented in Part 2 of my journey with Artjamila.

After all the hardships, the fruits of my labour prove to be fruitful. Jamila became an artist at the age of fourteen in 2016. And Jemima, my youngest daughter, became a writer, also at the age of fourteen in 2018. I hope that my journey and Jamila's creations of art become an inspiration to others. Life is a journey. Enjoy it.

Chapter 12

SELECTED EARLY YEARS SKETCHES WITH INTERPRETATIONS

In ancient times, cavemen used the technique of drawing on the walls of caves as a form of communication. Jamila seems to use this form of communication as well. She was non-verbal during her early years—from birth until six years of age. When she cannot gather the words, she uses drawing as a mode of communication. She draws her feelings of happiness, sadness, and anger on paper.

Early Years (E1: Happiness)

Early Years (E2: Sadness)

12-1:
Artist: Jamila
Title: *Happy*
Medium: Ink on paper
Year: 2012
Interpretation: Feeling happy

12-3:
Artist: Jamila
Title: *Sadness*
Medium: Ink on paper
Year: 2014
Interpretation: Feeling sad

Early Years (L2: Jamila Likes Beauty, Like Princess and Disney's Rapunzel)

12-5:
Artist: Jamila
Title: *Beautiful Women*
Medium: Ink on paper
Year: 2012
Interpretation: Beauty is Jamila's passion. Her drawings are inspired by women with long hair like princesses.

12-6
Artist: Jamila
Title: *Beautiful Women*
Medium: Pencil on paper
Year: 2010
Interpretation: Beauty is Jamila's passion. Her drawings are inspired by women with long hair like Disney's Rapunzel.

Early Years (L4: Jamila Likes Fashion and Modelling)

12-10:
Artist: Jamila
Title: *Fashion and Modelling*
Medium: Pencil on paper
Year: 2013
Interpretation: When she is happy, she is most likely to draw random fashion designs.

12-11:
Artist: Jamila
Title: *Fashion and Modelling*
Medium: Pencil on paper
Year: 2013
Interpretation: When she is happy, she is most likely to draw random fashion designs.

Early Years (M2: Jamila's Memories of the Dances at the School Concert)

12-14:
Artist: Jamila
Title: *Dance Concert*
Medium: Coloured pencil on paper
Year: 2013
Interpretation: Jamila's memories of the dances at the school concert

12-16:
Artist: Jamila
Title: *Dance Concert*
Medium: Ink on paper
Year: 2013
Interpretation: Jamila's memories of the dances at the school concert

12-17:
Artist: Jamila
Code: EY.M2.D13.2013
Title: *Dance Concert*
Medium: Ink on paper
Year: 2013
Interpretation: Jamila's memories of the dances at the school concert

Early Years (M4: Group Photo during Group Tour)

12-19:
Artist: Jamila
Title: *Group Photo during Group Tour*
Medium: Ink on paper
Year: 2012
Interpretation: Jamila's interpretation of group photos taken during her travels

Early Years (M6: Jamila's Memories of the Yearly Class Party at Primary School)

12-22:
Artist: Jamila
Title: *Schoolmates*
Medium: Coloured pencil on paper
Year: 2010
Interpretation: Jamila's schoolmates in her eyes

Early Years (M7: Jamila's Schoolmates in Her Eyes)

12-25:
Artist: Jamila
Title: *Schoolmates*
Medium: Ink on paper
Year: 2010
Interpretation: Jamila's schoolmates in her eyes

Early Years (M7: Jamila's Schoolmates in Her Eyes)

12-28:
Artist: Jamila
Title: *Schoolmates*
Medium: Ink on paper
Year: 2011
Interpretation: Jamila's schoolmates in her eyes

12-29:
Artist: Jamila
Title: *Schoolmates*
Medium: Ink on paper
Year: 2011
Interpretation: Jamila's schoolmates in her eyes

12-30:
Artist: Jamila
Title: *Schoolmates*
Medium: Ink on paper
Year: 2011
Interpretation: Jamila's schoolmates in her eyes

12-37:
Artist: Jamila
Title: *Schoolmates*
Medium: Ink on paper
Year: 2013
Interpretation: Jamila's schoolmates in her eyes

12-38:
Artist: Jamila
Title: *Schoolmates*
Medium: Ink on paper
Year: 2015
Interpretation: Jamila's schoolmates in her eyes

12-39:
Artist: Jamila
Title: *Schoolmates*
Medium: Pencil on paper
Year: 2015
Interpretation: Jamila's schoolmates in her eyes

12-40:
Artist: Jamila
Title: *Schoolmates*
Medium: Pencil on paper
Year: 2015
Interpretation: Jamila's schoolmates in her eyes

Early Years (M8: Family Activities)

12-51:
Artist: Jamila
Title: *Family Activities*
Medium: Pencil on paper
Year: 2010
Interpretation: Jamila's memories of family activities

12-53:
Artist: Jamila
Title: *Family Activities*
Medium: Ink on paper
Year: 2012
Interpretation: Jamila's memories of family activities

12-55:
Artist: Jamila
Title: *Family Activities*
Medium: Ink on paper
Year: 2012
Interpretation: Jamila's memories of family activities

12-54:
Artist: Jamila
Title: *Family Activities*
Medium: Ink on paper
Year: 2011
Interpretation: Jamila's memories of family activities

Chapter 13

SELECTED EARLY YEARS DIGITAL DRAWINGS WITH INTERPRETATIONS

Jamila overcame her stress and anxiety in 2012 through digitally drawing. She was not happy during standard 4 (in 2012). She felt alone in class, without a support teacher and bullied by her classmates. After some time, she installed an app on her tablet that allowed her to draw. The surprising thing is, she did it all by herself without any exposure to applications and downloading tutorials. She used her forefinger to draw, using her own style of drawing people's character. She has produced thousands of digital drawings using this technique. She revealed her feelings and emotions of happiness, sadness, and calmness through this media. She also documented her memories of school activities, friends, and family—activities like travelling and having tuition class at home. She also sketched everything she liked, such as beauty and fashion. Art is ultimately a therapeutic medium to release her stress, just like music.

Early Years (E1: Happiness)

13-1:
Artist: Jamila
Title: *Happy*
Medium: Digital drawing
Year: 2012
Interpretation: Feeling happy

13-2:
Artist: Jamila
Title: *Happy*
Medium: Digital drawing
Year: 2012
Interpretation: Feeling happy

13-3:
Artist: Jamila
Title: *Happy*
Medium: Digital drawing
Year: 2012
Interpretation: Feeling happy

Early Years (E2: Sadness)

13-9:
Artist: Jamila
Title: *Sadness*
Medium: Digital drawing
Year: 2012
Interpretation: Feeling sad

13-10:
Artist: Jamila
Title: Sadness
Medium: Digital Drawing
Year: 2012
Interpretation: Feeling sad

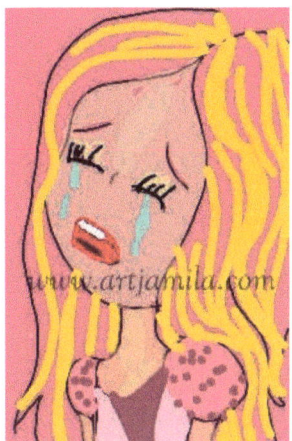

13-11:
Artist: Jamila
Title: *Sadness*
Medium: Digital drawing
Year: 2012
Interpretation: Feeling sad

Early Years (E3: Calm)

13-13:
Artist: Jamila
Title: *Calm*
Medium: Ink on paper
Year: 2013
Interpretation: A portrait that resembles Jamila's character (grace)

13-14:
Artist: Jamila
Title: *Calm*
Medium: Ink on paper
Year: 2013
Interpretation: A portrait that resembles Jamila's character (grace)

Early Years (L1: Jamila Likes Travel)

13-27:
Artist: Jamila
Title: *Jamila Likes Travel*
Medium: Digital
Year: 2013
Interpretation: This drawing shows Jamila's desire to travel on an aeroplane.

13-28:
Artist: Jamila
Title: *Jamila Likes Travel*
Medium: Digital
Year: 2013
Interpretation: This drawing shows Jamila's desire to travel.

13-29:
Artist: Jamila
Title: *Jamila Likes Travel*
Medium: Digital
Year: 2013
Interpretation: This drawing shows Jamila's desire to travel on an aeroplane.

13-30:
Artist: Jamila
Title: *Jamila Likes Travel*
Medium: Digital
Year: 2012
Interpretation: This drawing shows Jamila's desire to travel on public transportation, such as a monorail.

13-34:
Artist: Jamila
Title: *Jamila Likes Travel*
Medium: Digital
Year: 2013
Interpretation: This drawing shows Jamila's joy on a windy day during her travels.

13-36:
Artist: Jamila
Title: *Jamila Likes Travel*
Medium: Digital
Year: 2013
Interpretation: This drawing shows Jamila enjoyed her travel to KL Tower.

My Journey with Artjamila

13-37:
Artist: Jamila
Title: *Jamila Likes Travel*
Medium: Digital
Year: 2013
Interpretation: This drawing shows Jamila enjoys her travels under the rain with an umbrella.

13-38:
Artist: Jamila
Title: *Jamila Likes Travel*
Medium: Digital
Year: 2013
Interpretation: This drawing shows Jamila enjoys her travel to Penang.

13-41:
Artist: Jamila
Title: *Jamila Likes Travel*
Medium: Digital
Year: 2013
Interpretation: This drawing shows Jamila's desire to travel on an aeroplane.

Early Years (L2: Jamila Likes Beauty, Such as Princess and Disney's Rapunzel)

13-48:
Artist: Jamila
Title: *Beautiful Women*
Medium: Digital drawing
Year: 2012
Interpretation: Beauty is Jamila's passion. Her drawings are inspired by women with long hair like princesses.

13-50:
Artist: Jamila
Title: *Beautiful Women*
Medium: Digital drawing
Year: 2012
Interpretation: Beauty is Jamila's passion. Her drawings are inspired by women with long hair like princesses.

13-53:
Artist: Jamila
Code:
Title: *Beautiful Women*
Medium: Digital drawing
Year: 2012
Interpretation: Beauty is Jamila's passion. Her drawings are inspired by women with long hair like princesses.

Early Years (L4: Jamila Likes Fashion and Modelling)

13-60:
Artist: Jamila
Title: *Fashion and Modelling*
Medium: Digital drawing
Year: 2012
Interpretation: When she is happy, she is most likely to draw random fashion designs.

13-61:
Artist: Jamila
Title: *Fashion and Modelling*
Medium: Digital drawing
Year: 2012
Interpretation: When she is happy, she is most likely to draw random fashion designs.

13-62:
Artist: Jamila
Title: *Fashion and Modelling*
Medium: Digital drawing
Year: 2013
Interpretation: When she is happy, she is most likely to draw random fashion designs.

Early Years (M5: Jamila's Memories of Visits to Aquarium and Geological Parks—Fishes and Mermaids)

13-66:
Artist: Jamila
Title: *Visits to Aquarium*
Medium: Digital drawing
Year: 2012
Interpretation: An abstract piece of Jamila's memories during her visit to an aquarium

13-67:
Artist: Jamila
Title: *Visits to Aquarium*
Medium: Digital drawing
Year: 2012
Interpretation: An abstract piece of Jamila's memories during her visit to an aquarium

13-68:
Artist: Jamila
Title: *Visits to Aquarium Series FM40*
Medium: Digital drawing
Year: 2013
Interpretation: An abstract piece of Jamila's memories during her visit to an aquarium

Early Years (M6: Jamila's Memories of the Yearly Class Party at Primary School)

13-72:
Artist: Jamila
Title: *Class Party*
Medium: Digital drawing
Year: 2013
Interpretation: Jamila's memories of the yearly class party at school.

13-73:
Artist: Jamila
Title: *Class Party*
Medium: Digital drawing
Year: 2013
Interpretation: Jamila's memories of the yearly class party at school.

13-74:
Artist: Jamila
Title: *Class Party*
Medium: Digital drawing
Year: 2013
Interpretation: Jamila's memories of the yearly class party at school.

Early Years (M7: Jamila's Schoolmates in Her Eyes)

13-86:
Artist: Jamila
Title: *Schoolmates*
Medium: Digital drawing
Year: 2013
Interpretation: Jamila's schoolmates in her eyes

13-87:
Artist: Jamila
Title: *Schoolmates*
Medium: Digital drawing
Year: 2013
Interpretation: Jamila's locker number, 19, in the classroom

13-92:
Artist: Jamila
Title: *Schoolmates*
Medium: Digital drawing
Year: 2013
Interpretation: Jamila's schoolmates in her eyes

Early Years (M8: Family Activities)

13-100:
Artist: Jamila
Title: *Family Activities*
Medium: Digital drawing
Year: 2013
Interpretation: Jamila's memories of family activities

13-102:
Artist: Jamila
Title: *Family Activities*
Medium: Digital drawing
Year: 2013
Interpretation: Jamila's memories of family activities

13-103:
Artist: Jamila
Title: *Family Activities*
Medium: Digital drawing
Year: 2013
Interpretation: Jamila's memories of family activities

13-105:
Artist: Jamila
Code: EY.M8.FA31.DIGITAL.2013
Title: Family Activities
Medium: Digital Drawing
Year: 2013
Interpretation: Jamila's memories of family activities.

13-106:
Artist: Jamila
Code: EY.M8.FA27.DIGITAL.2013
Title: Family Activities
Medium: Digital Drawing
Year: 2013
Interpretation: Jamila's memories of family activities.

13-107:
Artist: Jamila
Code: EY.M8.FA36.DIGITAL.2013
Title: Family Activities
Medium: Digital Drawing
Year: 2013
Interpretation: Jamila's memories of family activities.

My Journey with Artjamila

13-108:
Artist: Jamila
Title: *Family Activities*
Medium: Digital drawing
Year: 2013
Interpretation: Jamila's memories of family activities

13-109:
Artist: Jamila
Title: *Family Activities*
Medium: Digital drawing
Year: 2013
Interpretation: Jamila's memories of family activities

13-110:
Artist: Jamila
Title: *Family Activities*
Medium: Digital drawing
Year: 2013
Interpretation: Jamila's memories of family activities

13-111:
Artist: Jamila
Title: *Family Activities*
Medium: Digital drawing
Year: 2013
Interpretation: Jamila's memories of family activities

13-112:
Artist: Jamila
Title: *Family Activities*
Medium: Digital drawing
Year: 2013
Interpretation: Jamila's memories of family activities

13-113:
Artist: Jamila
Title: *Family Activities*
Medium: Digital drawing
Year: 2013
Interpretation: Jamila's memories of family activities

Chapter 14

SELECTED RECENT PAINTINGS WITH INTERPRETATIONS

Three Ladies Series

14-2:
Artist: Jamila
Title: *Three Ladies Series 13B: Memories Are Golden*
Medium: Mixed media on canvas
Artwork: 610mm (W) x 762mm (H)
Frame: 863mm (W) x 1016mm (H)
Year: 2018
Country: Malaysia
Interpretation:
The most beautiful things are not associated with money. They are memories. Memories are the key to the future. Memories are treasures of the heart. Jamila loves travelling. Most of her travels during her childhood were with her mother and her younger sister. *Three Ladies* was inspired by those memories. Time is a blessing and *Memories Are Golden*.

14-8:
Artist: Jamila
Title: *Kebaya Girls Series 1*
Medium: Pigment ink on acid-free paper
Artwork: 280mm (W) x 200mm (H)
Frame: 508mm (W) x 459mm (H)
Year: 2016
Interpretation:
This drawing reflects Jamila's interest in fashion and modelling.

14-9:
Artist: Jamila
Code: RW.M7.SM2
Title: *Schoolmates Series 2*
Medium: Pigment ink on acid-free paper
Artwork: 270mm (W) x 200mm (H)
Frame: 508mm (W) x 458mm (H)
Year: 2016

Interpretation:
Jamila's multiracial schoolmates in her eyes

Noorhashimah Mohamed Noordin

Rapunzel Series

14-11:
Artist: Jamila
Title: *Rapunzel Series 5B*
Medium: Pigment Ink on acid-free paper
Artwork: 565mm (W) x 386mm (H)
Frame: 840mm (W) x 662mm (H)
Year: 2017

Beauty is Jamila's passion, and this drawing was inspired by women with long hair, mainly the Disney character Rapunzel. Rapunzel's magical long hair emphasises not only the amount of times she's been locked in the tower but also something divine—her ability to heal people who are hurt. Rapunzel reflects spiritual themes—our human instinct to heal; the imprisonment of our souls caused by deception and selfishness; our natural desire for freedom; and, above all, the power of love to motivate self-sacrifice for someone else. It is *A Reflection of Holistic Beauty*.

Mermaid Series

14-12:
Artist: Jamila
Title: *Mermaid Series 2: Life beyond Boundaries*
Medium: Mixed media on canvas
Artwork: 1193mm (W) x 430mm (H)
Frame: 1443mm (W) x 680mm (H)
Year: 2017
Country: Malaysia

Interpretation:
Mermaids are one of the most popular myths ever told in the history of legends. Commonly, they are portrayed as possessing girlish qualities and etiquette, providing for children gentle imaginations of mermaids. The mermaid reveals herself only to the special and those who truly understand her mystique. She is a beauty of unworldly measure who dances and explores the underwater world with no boundaries. Her graceful character touches innocent souls and hearts. She is a gift from the sea that reflects *Life beyond Boundaries*.

Basket Series

14-15:
Artist: Jamila
Title: *Basket Series 3: Weaving Our Dreams*
Medium: Acrylic 3D canvas
Artwork: 762mm (W) x 762mm (H)
Year: 2018
Country: Malaysia
Interpretation:
Jamila saw something in baskets. She saw them as something that held the energy of hard work poured into each bit of weaving material. Think of those materials as the creators' dreams, woven into something beautiful and useful to the lives of others. This says that one person's life can deeply inspire another.

Cats in Baskets Series

14-16:
Artist: Jamila
Title: *Cats in Baskets Series 2: "The Art of Togetherness"*
Medium: Acrylic on 3D canvas
Artwork: 305 mm (W) x 305 mm (H)
Total area of artwork: 395 mm (W) x 395mm (H)
Year: 2018
Country: Malaysia
Interpretation:
Cats are quite fascinating and adorable. Watching cats playing with woven baskets is fun and moves our emotion of happiness. The baskets reflect the energy of hard work poured into each bit of weaving material. A group of adorable cats playing together with the beautiful woven baskets reflects the *Art of Togetherness* in having fun.

Patriotic Series

14-20:
Artist: Jamila
Title: *Unity in Diversity Series 2*
Medium: Mix Media on Canvas
Artwork: 760 mm (W) x 1118 mm (H)
Frame: 1020 mm (W) x 1378 mm (H)
Year: 2017
Country: Malaysia
Interpretation:
As Malaysians, we all know the significance of 31 August 1957. It is the day our country marked its independence. More importantly, it's the day we began a new chapter in our history as a free nation. The assimilation of the five major ethnic groups in Malaysia (Malay, Chinese, Indian, Kadazan, and Iban) with the flying flags reflects the liberation of the mind and spirit of the people of Malaysia and sets the stage for the unleashing of full human potential and the drive for excellence. Apart from patriotism, these renderings of Malaysians from different walks of life and of different ages, races, and religions have a common objective—*unity*. This is what *Unity in Diversity* is all about. The background of buildings and infrastructure shows how much we have grown together as a nation.

14-21:
Artist: Jamila
Title: *Malaysian Flag Series 1*
Medium: Mixed media (acrylic on canvas and pigment ink on acrylic)
Artwork: 910mm (W) x 610 mm (H)
Frame: 1295mm (W x 991mm (H)
Year: 2017
Interpretation:
The assimilation of the three major ethnic groups (Malay, Chinese, and Indian) of people of Malaysia with the flying flag reflects *Unity in Diversity* of the mind and spirit of the people of Malaysia. The "Jalur Gemilang" is decorated with our national flower (*bunga raya*) in red and white. Malaysians from different walks of life and of different ages, races, and religions have a common objective—*unity*.

My Journey with Artjamila

Fish Mosaic Series

14-26:
Artist: Jamila
Title: *Fish Mosaic Series 9*
Medium: Pigment Ink on acid-free paper
Artwork: 420mm (W) x 220mm (H)
Frame: 600mm (W) x 400mm (H)
Year: 2017
Interpretation:
An abstract piece of Jamila's memories during her visit to an aquarium

14-31:
Artist: Jamila
Title: *Fish Mosaic Series 15: The Art of Togetherness*
Medium: Mixed media on 3D canvas
Artwork: 305mm (W) x 305mm (H)
Total area of artwork: 395mm (W) x 395mm (H)
Year: 2018
Country: Malaysia
Interpretation:
The *Fish Mosaic* series is a masterpiece of Jamila's memories of her visit to a world heritage geopark on the fascinating island of Langkawi in Malaysia called the Kilim Geological Park. Jamila draws her own interpretation of the different kinds of fish and marine creatures, clumping them together to show the art of togetherness. Her special inborn power of imagination and assimilation of patterns and colours in the fish mosaic makes her art different and unique. She has created a unique masterpiece of her memories in the form of collaged patterns of marine creatures.

Teapots Series

14-35:
Artist: Jamila
Title: *Teapot Series 1*
Medium: Pigment ink on acid-free paper
Artwork: 266mm (W) x 190mm (H)
Frame: 508mm (W) x 459mm (H)
Year: 2017
Interpretation:
Teapots carry a richer history than any other ceramic object in our household and are a symbol of potency. The astonishing variety of teapot shapes gives Jamila a sort of happiness no other object can rival. The pleasant taste of tea greatly inspires Jamila, and that inspiration is poured into her artwork, thus creating the *Teapots* series. Her observations of her surroundings, colours, and patterns of ornaments bleed onto her canvas at the stroke of her brush, creating works featuring teapots. In *Teapots,* she has created her own unique masterpiece of her sweet memories of enjoying hot tea.

14-38:
Artist: Jamila
Title: *Teapots Series 7: The Pleasant Taste of Tea*
Medium: Mixed media on 3D canvas
Artwork: 305mm (W) x 305mm (H)
Total area of artwork: 395mm (W) x 395mm (H)
Year: 2018
Country: Malaysia
Interpretation:
Teapots carry a richer history than any other ceramic object in our household and are a symbol of potency. The astonishing variety of teapot shapes gives Jamila a sort of happiness no other object can rival. The pleasant taste of tea greatly inspires Jamila, and that inspiration is poured into her artwork, thus creating the *Teapots* series. Her observations of her surroundings, colours, and patterns of ornaments bleed onto her canvas at the stroke of her brush, creating works featuring teapots. In *Teapots*, she has created her own unique masterpiece of her sweet memories of enjoying hot tea.

Butterfly Series

14-42:
Artist: Jamila
Title: *Butterflies Series 1: Flying High*
Medium: Mixed media on 3D canvas
Artwork: 305mm (W) x 305mm (H)
Total area of artwork: 395mm (W) x 395mm (H)
Year: 2018
Country: Malaysia
Interpretation:
They always say that the sky's your limit, and this painting is based on that notion. This quote has motivated Jamila quite a number of times along her journey to becoming the person she is today. Thinking of butterflies and how their flight is as free as their will to do so, Jamila uses butterflies as a metaphor—no matter how hard the wind blows your wings, you will still be able to catch yourself after falling 17 and aim higher again.

Dance Series

14-45:
Artist: Jamila
Title: *Malay Traditional Dance: Zapin, Malaysia Series 2*
Medium: Pigment ink on acid-free paper
Artwork: 295mm (W) x 206mm (H)
Frame: 420mm (W) x 320mm (H)
Year: 2016
Interpretation: Jamila's love for dancing motivated her to draw this painting.

Appendix

T-1:	....	Title page
A-1:	....	The footprints of my journey
A-2:	....	Jamila at 15 years old
A-3:	....	Jamila at 7 years old
A-4:	....	Jamila at 8 years old
A-5:	....	Jamila at 10 years old
A-6:	....	Jamila at 11 years old
A-7:	....	Jamila at 13 years old
A-8:	....	Jamila at 13 years old
A-9:	....	Jamila at 13 years old
A10:	....	Jamila at 14 years old with the crown prince of Selangor
A11:	....	Jamila at 15 years old with me at Bank Negara's charity exhibition
A-12:	....	Jamila at 15 years old in her art studio
A-13:	....	Jamila at 15 years old with Tan Sri Dato' Azman Hashim at Bank Negara exhibition
A-14:	....	Jamila at 15 years old at ArtEDecor exhibition in Matrade, KL, Malaysia
A15:	....	Jamila at 15 years old with the queen of Selangor at a charity exhibition by NASOM at Utropolis, Glenmarie, Selangor, Malaysia
A-16:	....	Jamila at 15 years old
1-2:	....	1 month old
1-3:	....	1 year old
1-9:	....	2 years old
1-12:	....	Sadness (Digital drawings by Jamila)
1-14:	....	Joy (Digital drawings by Jamila)
1-17:	....	Joy (Digital drawings by Jamila)
1-18:	....	Joy (Digital drawings by Jamila)
1-20:	....	Surprise (Digital drawings by Jamila)
1-21:	....	Boredom (Digital drawings by Jamila)
1-23:	....	As a lecturer (associate professor in a local university (UiTM)
1-24:	....	As a speaker at "PAM" for Part III Professional Examination Workshop
1-25:	....	As part of LAM Part III Professional Examination Committee
1-26:	....	As a principal to Noorhashima, Noordin Architect
1-27:	....	Managing projects at site
1-28:	....	Managing projects and managing a sole proprietor company
1-29:	....	Dr Norizan Rajak
1-30:	....	Jamila at preschool in 2008 when she was 6 years old
1-31:	....	Jamila at preschool in 2008 when she was 6 years old
1-32:	....	Jamila at preschool in 2008 when she was 6 years old
1-33:	....	Jamila at preschool in 2008 when she was 6 years old
2-1:	....	Mr Lee Peng Chiong
2-3:	....	Standard 1 (2008 primary school)
2-5:	....	Standard 1 (2008 primary school)
2-6:	....	Standard 1 (2008 primary school)
2-7:	....	Standard 1 (2008 primary school)
2-8:	....	Standard 1 (2008 primary school)
2-9:	....	Drawings by Jamila showing an event at school
2-13:	....	Drawings by Jamila showing an event at school
2-14:	....	Sum Mooi Soo

2-15:	....	Noorsa'adah Mohd Noordin
2-16:	....	Jamila sees things in three-dimensional form
2-17:	....	Jamila at primary school
2-19:	....	Jamila at primary school
2-21:	....	Jamila at primary school
2-23:	....	Compilation of expressed notes from bookstores (mathematics)
2-24:	....	Compilation of expressed notes from bookstores (science)
2-25:	....	Compilation of my research and studies into lecture notes
2-27:	....	Study room at home
2-28:	....	Study room at home
2-32:	....	Study room at home
2-33:	....	My office in my architectural firm
2-34:	....	Kids study room attached to principal room
2-35:	....	Kids tuition room attached to principal room
2-36:	....	Class revision at school during December school holiday by Noorhashimah Noordin
2-37:	....	Class revision at school during December school holiday by Noorhashimah Noordin
2-38:	....	The standard government school's curriculum structure for mathematics
2-39:	....	Modular system curriculum structure for mathematics without limitation of time for each module
2-40:	....	The modular system for mathematics (division by Noorhashimah Noordin)
2-41:	....	Teaching using conventional method by writing on the board
2-42:	....	Teaching using technology by Noorhashimah Noordin
2-43:	....	The modular system for mathematics (multiplication) by Noorhashimah Noordin
2-44:	....	Teaching using conventional method by writing on paper by Noorhashimah Noordin
2-45:	....	Interactive teaching method on movable white board with miniature clocks
2-46:	....	Mind mapping for science subject
2-47:	....	Mind mapping for science subject
2-48:	....	Modelling of farm animals for science subject
2-49:	....	Experiment for science subject
2-50:	....	Teaching process of painting for art subject
2-51:	....	Painting with crayon technique by Jamila
2-52:	....	Watercolour technique by Jamila
2-53:	....	Jamila with her iPad doing digital drawings
2-56:	....	Digital drawings by Jamila
2-57:	....	Miss Judith Anthony
2-58:	....	Jamila (second from right) and Jemima (third from right), 2013
2-59:	....	Jamila (standing at the centre), 2013
2-60:	....	Drawing by Jamila in her school exercise book—*The Team Rainbow Dash*, 2013
2-61:	....	Drawing by Jamila titled *People of Malaysia*, 2013
2-64:	....	Jamila draws all the dance activities of the school concert from her memory, 2013
2-65:	....	School concert, Jamila at far right (2013)
2-66:	....	School concert, Jamila at far right (2013)
2-67:	....	Jamila (Far left, front line) with schoolmates during UPSR examination briefing by the school's principal (2015)
3-1:	....	Sketches of the dance steps drawn from Jamila's memory when she gets home from school, 2013
3-2:	....	Sketches of the dance drawn from Jamila's memory when she gets home from the school concert, 2013
3-3:	....	Jamila doing mural painting, 2017
3-4:	....	Jamila in her art studio
3-5:	....	Jamila in her art studio
3-6:	....	Jamila in her art studio
3-7:	....	Educational approach by Noorhashimah Noordin

3-8:	....	Educational route by Noorhashimah Noordin
3-9:	....	Homeschool curriculum structure by Noorhashimah Noordin
3-11:	....	Group exhibition (IACON)
3-13:	....	Group exhibition (Avenue K)
3-15:	....	Group exhibition (The Ledge Gallery)
3-16:	....	Solo exhibition (Concorde Hotel, Shah Alam, Selangor, Malaysia)
3-17:	....	The crown prince of Selangor visited Jamila's exhibition and signed Jamila's painting
3-18:	....	Group exhibition at PAM.
3-20:	....	Group exhibition (The Ledge Gallery)
3-23:	....	Critique session at Sha Alam Art Gallery
3-24:	....	Montessori Forum at Kuala Lumpur, Malaysia (2017)
3-26:	....	Art Bazaar at Bank Negara Malaysia
3-35:	....	Imago Mundi 3 Nation
3-38:	....	ArtEDecor, Matrade, KL, Malaysia
3-39:	....	ArtEDecor, Matrade, KL, Malaysia
3-45:	....	NASOM exhibition. Formal visit by the queen of Selangor (second from left)
3-52:	....	Live drawing at TV station, TV9, KL, Malaysia
3-54:	....	Live painting at TV station, TV1, KL, Malaysia
3-55:	....	Live mural painting at SMK Seksyen 9, Shah Alam, Selangor, Malaysia
3-56:	....	Live mural painting at SMK Seksyen 9, Shah Alam, Selangor, Malaysia
3-58:	....	Live drawing in a sharing session seminar at Manipal Hospital, Selangor, Malaysia
3-59:	....	Live painting event, "Malaysia Makes History"
3-62:	....	Live painting at SMK Danau Kota, KL, Malaysia
3-64:	....	Merdeka live painting officiated by the deputy minister of tourism in Malaysia
3-68:	....	Live painting competition at National Art Gallery, KL, Malaysia
3-70:	....	Live painting competition at National Art Gallery, KL, Malaysia
3-71:	....	Press conference with *Kosmo!* newspaper
3-73:	....	Press conference with group of reporters brought by Selangor Economic Planning Unit (UPEN)
3-77:	....	Tour to exhibitions by others
3-85:	....	Entertaining visitors at gallery
3-88:	....	The art of cooking roti jala
3-90:	....	The art of cooking roti jala
3-91:	....	The art of cooking roti jala
3-92:	....	The art of cooking roti jala
3-95:	....	The art of cooking, preparation onions
3-96:	....	The art of cooking, frying onions
3-97:	....	Baking
3-98:	....	Baking
3-99:	....	Baking
3-100:	....	Baking
3-101:	....	Baking
3-103:	....	Organising kitchen utensils
3-104:	....	Organising kitchen utensils
3-105:	....	Organising kitchen utensils
3-106:	....	Organising kitchen utensils
3-107:	....	Organising kitchen utensils
3-109:	....	Organising mattress
3-112:	....	Opening all doors and windows
3-115:	....	Laundry routine
3-117:	....	Laundry routine

3-123: .... Laundry
3-126: .... Laundry
3-127: .... Preparing breakfast
3-128: .... Preparing breakfast
3-130: .... Preparing breakfast
3-133: .... Grooming
3-135: .... Daily painting activity in art studio
3-144: .... Sharing session at Manipal Hospital
3-145: .... Sharing session at Manipal Hospital
3-146: .... Sharing session at Manipal Hospital
3-149: .... Sharing session at SMK Danau Kota, KL, Malaysia
3-150: .... Sharing session at International Montessori Forum
3-151: .... Sharing session at International Montessori Forum
3-152: .... Sharing session at International Montessori Forum
3-153: .... Sharing session at Manipal Hospital
3-154: .... Sharing session at Manipal Hospital
3-155: .... Sharing session at Manipal Hospital
3-156: .... Sharing session at SC Malaysia
3-157: .... Sharing session at SC Malaysia
3-158: .... Sharing session at SC Malaysia
4-1: .... Early years digital drawing (*Beautiful Women Series B45*)
4-2: .... Recent work (*Anora Series 1B*)
4-3: .... Early years digital drawing (*Beautiful Women Series B12*)
4-4: .... Recent work (*Rapunzel Series 5B*)
4-5: .... Early years digital drawing (*Family Activities Series FA28*)
4-6: .... Recent work (*Teapots Series 7, The Pleasant Taste of Tea*)
4-7: .... Early years digital drawing (*Fashion and modelling Series F14*)
4-8: .... Recent work (*Kebaya Girls Series 1*)
4-9: .... Early years ink on art paper (*Dance Concert Series D11*)
4-10: .... Recent work (Malay Traditional Dance, *Zapin Series 2*)
4-11: .... Early years digital drawing (*Flowers Series 1*)
4-12: .... Recent work (*Orchid Flowers Series 1*)
4-13B: .... Early years digital drawing (*Three Ladies Series TL44*)
4-14: .... Recent work (*Three Ladies in Kebaya Series 2B*)
4-15: .... Early years sketches of ink on art paper (*Multiracial People* Series 1)
4-16: .... Recent work (*Schoolmates Series 2*)
4-17: .... Early years ink on paper (*Group Photo During Group Tours Series GT1*)
4-18: .... Recent work (*Group Photo During Her Travels Series 1*)
4-19B: .... Early years digital drawing (*Visit to Aquarium Series FM2*)
4-20: .... Recent work (*Fish Mosaic Series 10 "The Art of Togetherness"*)
4-21B: .... .Early years digital drawing (*Visit to Aquarium Series FM1*)
4-22: .... Recent work (*Mermaids Series 2 "Life Beyond Boundaries"*)
4-23: .... Early years digital drawing (*Schoolmates Series SM39*)
4-24: .... Recent work (*Schoolmates Series 1*)
4-25: .... Early years digital drawing (*Family Activities Series FA26*)
4-26: .... Recent work (*Cats in Baskets Series 2,"The Art of Togetherness"*)
4-27: .... Early years digital drawing (*Butterflies Series 1*)
4-28: .... Recent work (*Butterflies Series 1 "Flying High"*)
4-29: .... Picture of cat in bed, Smokey
4-29B: .... Picture of cat in bed, Smokey

4-30:	....	Recent work (*Cats in Pyjamas Series 1*)
4-31:	....	Picture of Independence Day celebration (Merdeka at primary school
4-31B:	....	Picture of school parade in primary school
4-32:	....	Early years sketches *(Schoolmates SM22)*
4-33:	....	Recent work, *Unity in Diversity Series 2)*
4-34:	....	Picture of Malaysian people waving the Malaysian flag during Independence Day celebration
4-34B:	....	Picture of Malaysian people carrying Malaysian flag
4-35:	....	Recent work, *(Malaysian Flag Series 1)*
5-1:	....	Jamila in art studio
5-2:	....	Brochure exhibition ArtEDecor at Malaysia Trade Centre (Matrade)
5-3:	....	*Gaya Travel* (2017), "Selangor's Passion Expressed through Crafts from the Heart"
5-4:	....	*Iris*, (January 2018), "Young Artist With Big Talent"
5-5:	....	Star Media Group's *Kuntum*. (April 2018) "The Magical Touch of Jamila"
5-6:	....	.DBP Magazine April 2018), "Young Autistic Girl: A Shining Star in the Sky"
5-7:	....	26 March 2017, TV9 Kopitiam (Live painting: *Three Ladies Series 5A*)
5-8:	....	11 July 2017, TV1, SPM (Live painting: *Unity in Diversity Series 1: Malaysian Flag*)
5-9:	....	7 April 2018, TV3, Borak Kopitiam (Painting: *Cats in Baskets*)
5-10:	....	5 January 2018, TV3, Malaysia Hari Ini (a documentary by TV3)
5-11:	....	5 January 2018, TV3, Malaysia Hari Ini (a documentary by TV3)
5-12:	....	*Kosmo!* 3 April 2017, "Amateur Autistic Artist with Big Talent"
5-13:	....	*Kosmo!* 14 August 2017
5-14:	....	*Kosmo!* 14 August 2017, "Wan Jamila's Empire of Art"
5-15:	....	*Malay Mail*, 14 August 2017, "Merdeka Theme Brings out Best in Artist"
5-16:	....	*Malay Mail*, 20 September 2017, "Speaking through Art"
5-17:	....	*Fish Mosaic Series 10: The Art of Togetherness*
6-1:	....	*Three Ladies Series 2B*
6-2:	....	Dato Salleh Yeop
6-3:	....	*Three Ladies in Kimono Series 9B*
6-3B:	....	*Rapunzel Series 3B*
6-4:	....	Mizuan Abdul Manaf
6-5:	....	Three Ladies in Kebaya Series
6-6:	....	TPr. Hj. Ihsan Zainal Mokhtar
6-7:	....	*Three Ladies Series 7B*
6-8:	....	Ar. Datuk Tan Pei Ing
6-9:	....	*Three Ladies in Kebaya Series 11B*
6-10:	....	Dato' Dr Zalizan Mohd Jelas
6-11:	....	*Rapunzel Series 2B*
6-12:	....	*Teapots Series 2*
6-13:	....	*Teapots Series 1*
6-14:	....	*Three Ladies Series 5B*
6-15:	....	*Fish Mosaic Series 1*
6-16:	....	*Malay Traditional Dance, Ulek Mayang, Malaysia. Series 1*
6-17:	....	*Chinese Traditional Dance, Fan Dance, Malaysia Series 1*
6-18:	....	*Three Ladies in Kimono Series 10B*
6-19:	....	*Malay Traditional Dance, Zapin, Malaysia Series 1*
6-20:	....	*Group Photo During Travels Series 2*
6-21:	....	*Malay Traditional Dance, Gamelan, Malaysia Series 1*
6-22:	....	*Three Ladies Series 3B*
6-23:	....	Corporate Painting MBSB
6-24:	....	Azlina Mohd Rashad

6-25:	*Mermaid Series 3: Life beyond Boundaries*
6-26:	*Fish Mosaic Series 14: The Art of Togetherness*
6-27:	*Fish Mosaic Series 15: The Art of Togetherness*
6-28:	*Fish Mosaic Series 16: The Art of Togetherness*
6-29:	*Teapots Series 6: The Pleasant Taste of Tea*
6-30:	*Teapots Series 7: The Pleasant Taste of Tea*
6-31:	*Teapots Series 8: The Pleasant Taste of Tea*
6-32:	*Butterflies Series 2 Flying High*
6-33:	*Cats in Pyjamas Series 1*
6-34:	*Cats in Pyjamas Series 2*
6-35:	*The Dance Series 1*
6-36:	*Orchid Series 1*
6-37:	*Cats in Baskets Series 2: The Art of Togetherness*
6-38:	*Cats in Baskets Series 1: The Art of Togetherness*
6-39:	Rosli Mohd Rose
6-43:	*Fish Mosaic Series 13: The Art of Togetherness*
6-44:	Zaiton Jamaluddin
6-45:	*Fish Mosaic Series 12*
6-46:	Alice Chang Oi Lai
6-47:	*Rapunzel Series 3B*
6-48:	Charlie Yap
6-49:	*Baskets Series 2: Weaving Our Dreams.*
6-50:	Ar. Hazlinda Hashim
6-51:	*Fish Mosaic Series 11*
6-52:	Tan Sri Dato' Azman Hashim
7-1:	Zuriyadi Sarpin
7-2:	Wan Muhammad Danial Wan Omar
7-3:	Nor Azmi Sulong
7-4:	Lum Peng Cheong
8-1:	Khalid Mohd Sapari
8-2:	Nur Azmi Mokhtar
8-3:	Jamal Tommy
8-4:	Wan Borhanuddin Md Noor
8-5:	Zaharin Mohammad
8-6:	Abey Zoul
8-7:	Rizalman Misran (Ryzal Mysran)
8-8:	Nor Hanem Mohd Nor
8-9:	Abdullah Harun
8-10:	Abu Zaki Hadri
8-11:	Mazlan Noor Along.
9-1:	*The Malaysian Flag Series 1*
9-2:	Maheswari Thanapalasingam
9-3:	Dr Ralph Richard Klemp
9-4:	Ar. Lillian Tay
9.5:	*Fish Mosaic Series 4*
9-6:	Jumie Al Idid
9-7:	May Ki Wong
9-8:	Ruby Ann Phillip
9-9:	Hishamuddin Mohamed
10-1:	Yasmin Kassim

10-2: .... Ar. Associate Professor (Retired Ong Suan Huah)
10-3: .... Sum Mooi Soo
10-4: .... Associate Professor Sr Hasmawati Harun CQS
10-5: .... Munirah Abd Mutalib
10-6: .... Dr Imanul Hassan Abdul Shukor
10-7: .... 2 September 2007 Jemima (4), Jamila (5)
10-8: .... 8 September 2007 Jemima (4), Jamila (5)
10-9: .... 8 September 2007 Jemima (4), Jamila (5)
10-10: .... 1 October 2008 Jemima (5), Jamila (6)
10-11: .... 29 May 2009 Jemima (6), Jamila (7)
10-12: .... 29 May 2009 Jemima (6), Jamila (7)
10-13: .... 23 September 2009 Jemima (6), Jamila (7)
10-14: .... 15 May 2010 Jemima (7), Jamila (8)
10-15: .... 19 June 2010 Jemima (7), Jamila (8)
10-16: .... 10 November 2012 Jemima (9), Jamila (10)
10-17: .... 10 November 2012 Jemima (9), Jamila (10)
10-18: .... 15 January 2012 Jemima (9), Jamila (10)
11-1: .... The footprints of my journey
11-2: .... *Three Ladies Series 13B: Memories Are Golden*
11-3: .... *Cats in Basket Series 2: The Art of Togetherness*
11-4: .... Anora Series 1B
11-5: .... *Cats in Pyjamas Series 1*
11-13: .... Jamila at 15 years old
11-16: .... Jamila at 15 years old
12-1: .... Early Years (*E1: Happiness*)
12-3: .... Early Years (*E2: Sadness*
12-5: .... Early Years (*L2: Beauty Like Princess and Rapunzel from Disney*)
12-6: .... Early Years (*L2: Beauty Like Princess and Rapunzel from Disney*)
12-10: .... Early Years (*L4: Jamila Likes Fashion and Modelling*)
12-11: .... Early Years (*L4: Jamila Likes Fashion and Modelling*)
12-14: .... Early Years (*L4: Jamila Likes Fashion and Modelling*)
12-16: .... Early Years (*M2: Jamila's Memories on the Dances in the School Concert*)
12-17: .... Early Years (*M2: Jamila's Memories on the Dances in the School Concert*)
12-19: .... Early Years (Group photo during group tour)
12-22: .... Early Years (*M6: Jamila's Memories on the Yearly Class Party at Primary School*)
12-25: .... Early Years (*M7: Jamila's Schoolmates in Her Eyes*)
12-28: .... Early Years (*M7: Jamila's Schoolmates in Her Eyes*)
12-29: .... Early Years (*M7: Jamila's Schoolmates in Her Eyes*)
12-30: .... Early Years (*M7: Jamila's Schoolmates in Her Eyes*)
12-37: .... Early Years (*M7: Jamila's Schoolmates in Her Eyes*)
12-38: .... Early Years (*M7: Jamila's Schoolmates in Her Eyes*)
12-39: .... Early Years (*M7: Jamila's Schoolmates in Her Eyes*)
12-40: .... Early Years (*M7: Jamila's Schoolmates in Her Eyes*)
12-51: .... Early Years (*M8: Family Activities*)
12-53: .... Early Years (*M8: Family Activities*)
12-54: .... Early Years (*M8: Family Activities*)
12-55: .... Early Years (*M8: Family Activities*)
13-1: .... Early Years (*E1: Happiness*)
13-2: .... Early Years (*E1: Happiness*)
13-3: .... Early Years (*E1: Happiness*)

13-9: .... Early Years (*E2: Sadness*)
13-10: .... Early Years (*E2: Sadness*)
13-11: .... Early Years (*E2: Sadness*)
13-13: .... Early Years (*E3: Calm*)
13-14: .... Early Years (*E3: Calm*)
13-27: .... Early Years (*L1: Jamila Likes Travel*)
13-28: .... Early Years (*L1: Jamila Likes Travel*)
13-29: .... Early Years (*L1: Jamila Likes Travel*)
13-30: .... Early Years (*L1: Jamila Likes Travel*)
13-34: .... Early Years (*L1: Jamila Likes Travel*)
13-36: .... Early Years (*L1: Jamila Likes Travel*)
13-37: .... Early Years (*L1: Jamila Likes Travel*)
13-38: .... Early Years (*L1: Jamila Likes Travel*)
13-41: .... Early Years (*L1: Jamila Likes Travel*)
13-48: .... Early Years (*L2: Jamila Likes Beauty like Princesses and Rapunzel from Disney*)
13-50: .... Early Years (*L2: Jamila Likes Beauty like Princesses and Rapunzel from Disney*)
13-53: .... Early Years (*L2: Jamila Likes Beauty like Princesses and Rapunzel from Disney*)
13-60: .... Early Years (*L4: Jamila Likes Fashion and Modelling*)
13-61: .... Early Years (*L4: Jamila Likes Fashion and Modelling*)
13-62: .... Early Years (*L4: Jamila Likes Fashion and Modelling*)
13-66: .... Early Years (*M5: Jamila's Memories on Visits to Aquarium and Geological Parks*)
13-67: .... Early Years (*M5: Jamila's Memories on Visits to Aquarium and Geological Parks*)
13-68: .... Early Years (*M5: Jamila's Memories on Visits to Aquarium and Geological Parks*)
13-72: .... Early Years (*M6: Jamila's Memories on the Yearly Class Party at Primary School*)
13-73: .... Early Years (*M6: Jamila's Memories on the Yearly Class Party at Primary School*)
13-74: .... Early Years (*M6: Jamila's Memories on the Yearly Class Party at Primary School*)
13-86: .... Early Years (*M7: Jamila's Schoolmates in Her Eyes*)
13-87: .... Early Years (*M7: Jamila's Schoolmates in Her Eyes*)
13-92: .... Early Years (*M7: Jamila's Schoolmates in Her Eyes*)
13-100: .... Early Years (*M8: Family Activities Early Years*)
13-102: .... Early Years (*M8: Family Activities Early Years*)
13-103: .... Early Years (*M8: Family Activities Early Years*)
13-105: .... Early Years (*M8: Family Activities Early Years*)
13-106: .... Early Years (*M8: Family Activities Early Years*)
13-107: .... Early Years (*M8: Family Activities Early Years*)
13-108: .... Early Years (*M8: Family Activities Early Years*)
13-109: .... Early Years (*M8: Family Activities Early Years*)
13-110: .... Early Years (*M8: Family Activities Early Years*)
13-111: .... Early Years (*M8: Family Activities Early Years*)
13-112: .... Early Years (*M8: Family Activities Early Years*)
13-113: .... Early Years (*M8: Family Activities Early Years*)
14-2: .... *Three Ladies* Series
14-8: .... *Kebaya Girls* Series
14-9: .... *Kebaya Girls* Series
14-11: .... *Rapunzel* Series
14-12: .... *Mermaids* Series
14-15: .... *Basket* Series
14-16: .... *Cats in Baskets* Series
14-20: .... *Patriotic* Series
14-21: .... *Patriotic* Series

14-26: .... *Fish Mosaic* Series
14-31: .... *Fish Mosaic* Series
14-35: .... *Teapot* Series
14-38: .... *Teapot* Series
14-42: .... *Butterfly* Series
14-45: .... *Dance* Series
B-1: .... Noorhashimah Noordin (mother and writer)
B-2: .... Jemima Shaiful (co-writer)
B-3: .... Jamila (artist: Artjamila)
A-1: .... The footprints of my journey

About the Authors and the Artist

B-1:
Noorhashimah Noordin
Writer (mother of Jamila and art manager of Artjamila)

Ar. Associate Professor (Retired) Noorhashimah Mohamed Noordin is a professional architect and was an associate professor at UiTM as part of the faculty of architecture. She is also active on numerous professional platforms. She ran her own company (Noorhashima.N.Noordin Architect) and served on the board of architects as LAM Part 3 Professional Examination Council Member and on the committee of LAM Part 3 Professional Examination. Despite her busy schedule as an architect and associate professor, Noorhashimah personally taught her autistic daughter at home daily after school and on weekends. Her efforts proved fruitful when Jamila managed to sit for UPSR (the government elementary examination at the age of thirteen) in 2015 and became an artist at the age of fourteen in 2016. After Noorhashimah recovered from two major operations she underwent upon being diagnosed with cancer, she decided to retire from all her multiple professional duties and became an art manager of Artjamila.

B-2:
Jemima Shaiful
Co-Writer (younger sister of Jamila)

Wan Jemima Wan Shaiful Bahri was born on the 18 September 2003. She is the youngest in a family of five siblings. Since a very young age, she demonstrated her independence and has a mind of her own. She was able to carry the burden of responsibility of looking after her elder sister, Wan Jamila, in school, even in primary school. Wan Jemima is a voracious reader, sometimes going through two novels at a time. She also has an interest in writing and has BEEN encouraged at school and at home to nurture this interest. She is an introverted person and is currently (during the first half of 2018) attending an international school at level 9; she will be attending level 10 during the second half of the year. At the age of fourteen in 2018 she became a co-writer of *My Journey with Artjamila, Part 1*.

B-3:
Jamila (Artjamila)
(Artist)

Wan Jamila Wan Shaiful Bahri was born in Kuala Lumpur, Malaysia, on 13 June 2002. She was diagnosed as autistic at the age of four. Since the age of four, she has used drawings, as a way of revealing her feelings of happiness, sadness, and anger. Wan Jamila is now an artist with special talent. She received coaching from her mother since she was ten. From the age of fourteen onwards, several local artists provided guidance to her and her mother on the technical aspects of fine art. Jamila became a true artist at the age of fourteen. She draws intricate patterns and human expressions based on her experiences and observations, as well as her own interpretation of people. Her special inborn power of imagination and assimilation of patterns and colours makes her art different and unique. Most of her drawings are a collection of her memories in terms of her emotions, her passions, and events she experienced. She created a unique masterpiece of her memories in the form of collaged patterns. Her series of masterpieces are *Three Ladies, Triple Erato, Kebaya Girls, Rapunzel, Anora, Fish Mosaic, Teacups, Mermaids, Unity in Diversity* (*Merdeka* and *People of Malaysia*), *Cats, Butterflies, Cats in Baskets,* and many others. Each of her drawings delivers a message. One of these is: "Life is all about making memories. Today's little moments become tomorrow's unforgettable experiences."

Email: artjamila2002@gmail.com
Mobile: +6019-3152662
Website: www.artjamila.com
Fb page: https://www.facebook.com/artjamilapage.com
Fb: https://www.facebook.com.artjamila2002
Ig: https://www.Instagram.com/artjamila